THE MAKINGS OF A
MILLIONAIRE
MIND

Building a Life of
Abundance and Wealth

DANIEL GOMEZ

Daniel Gomez Enterprises, LLC

The Makings of a Millionaire Mind
Building a Life of Abundance and Wealth

Written by Daniel Gomez

Published by Daniel Gomez Enterprises LLC / April 2022
Copyright © 2022, Daniel Gomez
ISBN: 9798449156235

Printed in the United States of America

TABLE OF CONTENTS

PART 1:
BECOMING A MILLIONAIRE

PART 2:
THE MONEY FILES

PART 3:
BUILD YOUR MILLIONAIRE LIFE

INTRODUCTION

I want to say "Thank You" for purchasing this copy of *The Makings of a Millionaire Mind* book. I want to say "Thank You" for taking a chance and investing in yourself.

Most people, as adults, never invest in themselves after their high school graduation. They never pick up a book or put any effort into their personal growth or into themselves.

But **YOU!**

You are different!

You are a winner!

You were born to make millions!

It may have been the title of this book that piqued your interest. It may have been recommended by a friend or colleague. I really want to say "Thank You" from the bottom of my heart. In this book, you're going to learn many wealth principles, success principles and prosperity principles that are going to change your life and business!

Have you ever wondered why some people get richer and richer and for others, no matter how hard they work, they never get over that hump? They never achieve success, whatever that may mean to them. They are living paycheck-to-paycheck and struggling which is the sad truth in our country here in America, but it is reality.

I want to encourage you as you read these pages, I really want you to open up your heart because something magical happens when you do. It opens up your mind and you are ready to receive and download deep into your subconscious mind the wisdom that is in this book.

I want you to read this book as if you are going to teach it. Yes, you heard me right! Read this book if you are the one who is going to teach it because this will help you retain more of the information, a lot more the wisdom that is within these pages. I encourage you to get out a pen, some paper, and a highlighter. As you're reading this, take your time and do not rush through this book. I really want you to soak in all the principles and all the wisdom this book holds.

As you read, use this book as a coloring book. Highlight it all over the place! I want you to take notes. I really want you to study this because when you truly approach this information as a student, the real shift in your thinking is going to happen. Your breakthrough is right around the corner.

Most people are broke, poor, and struggling in life because they have the wrong relationship with money. I want you to change your thoughts. I want to change your mindset about money. It's time you change your beliefs and understand that money is good for you.

Money in itself is not bad. Money is simply paper with ink on it. But many of us are scared to even talk about money or just bring it up in a conversation. We think it is evil or we have learned those lies that we heard as a child. We have a belief system in our mind which we learned as children, that money is the root of all evil and that whoever has money is greedy and wicked. In our heart, many of us still believe this to be true.

Ponder on this for a moment. What have you believed to be true but is actually a lie? Most of us have inherited or adopted the belief systems and the relationships we have with money from our parents. The same way we inherit our DNA from our mom and dad, we also inherit their "financial DNA", their financial inner-economy template.

If your parents have a poor-minded inner economy, there's a great likelihood that you're going to have a poor-minded financial inner-economy. But if you inherit their wealthy man's DNA, the odds of you being wealthy and prosperous are in your favor!

Think about it for a moment.

Have you ever wondered why some people always have money problems? No matter what they do, things don't go right. They always seem to have financial challenges. We are going to discuss all of those things here in *The Makings of a Millionaire Mind*. You are going to open up your mind and your perspective to new ways of thinking.

Do me a favor, and as you start to read this book, I want you to approach it without judgment, without any bias. Just be open-minded. Yes, it is that simple. Be open-minded.

As you go through these chapters and pages, I feel that some principles are going to speak louder to you than others. Grab a hold of the ones that speak to your heart and soul and use them to guide you along your own unique path.

Many times, I've heard in conferences, seminars, workshops, and from various coaches that I needed to develop a millionaire mindset. My path was unique to me. In this book, I am going to share with you what took me from being a child that ate cereal with water (because we couldn't afford the milk) to being the successful multi-millionaire that I am today.

It has not been easy. I have cried. I have wanted to quit many times. I wanted to give up. Something deep down inside of me would not allow me to. I knew I was destined to write this book to help thousands of people who grew up living paycheck-to-paycheck, who heard from their parents they couldn't afford the things they wanted, who were always asked, "Do you think money grows on trees?"

Well, today is a new day for you and your family. You will change the direction of your family tree with a brand-new lineage for your household. You will start a new legacy. From this day forward, as you read this book, your thoughts are going to begin to elevate, you're going to think much bigger and your whole money paradigm will change.

In order for your bank account to grow, you must grow. You must change your relationship with money. You must change how you use money and you must change your relationship with yourself. What do I mean by that? If we have a poor self-image, we will never have an image of abundance and wealth and of prosperity. Please take this to heart.

I am proof that it can be done. I have been working on myself for many years. I had to challenge the old Daniel Gomez, the broke Daniel Gomez, the poor-minded Daniel Gomez many times. Every time I reached a new level of success, it seemed I had to dig deeper in order to reach the next level of success.

Brace yourself for an amazing journey! This journey of going from a poor-minded financial inner economy to a millionaire's financial inner economy is a process. I call it "a journey of becoming."

You are becoming more.

Be kind to yourself, don't beat yourself up. Have fun along the way! I know that you are reading this book for a reason, for a purpose. Something intrigued you about it. I want you to know this: you were not created to be poor. You were not created to be an average citizen. When God created you, he created you to do amazing things. He created you for a purpose. He created you to make an impact in this world.

Before we begin this journey, do me a favor. Place your right hand over your heart. Yes, really do this. Place your right hand over your heart. Do you feel that? Do you feel that heartbeat right now? I do. That means you are reading this book for a reason and it is much bigger than yourself. Wealth has allowed me to help other people. Wealth has allowed me to be more, do more and have more. It brings me great joy to help those around me.

I am no better than you. I know that if God can use me, He can use you. You were born to succeed. You were born for greatness. You were born to be a millionaire. Yes, you heard me! Maybe you have never heard anybody call you that or tell you that.

 As a matter of fact, take your pen and paper and write this down: "I am a millionaire. I am a multi-millionaire. I was born to make millions!" Write down those "Millionaire Affirmations." Start with these three.

When I am coaching my clients and I ask them to do this exercise, they struggle to say it because these words have never come out of their mouths. They've never heard these words growing up as a child or anywhere else for that matter.

Today I'm going to challenge you to believe more for yourself. Many times, we believe things like this for the person on the other side of the room but sadly many of us do not believe this for ourselves. This is possible for you. Yes! Becoming a millionaire is possible for you! Say that! Say it out loud right now.

"I was born to make millions!" People might think you are crazy. People might think you have lost your mind. But it is okay! They don't complain when the check comes for dinner and you have the money to pay it. It allows us to be a blessing to the people around us.

For some of you reading this introduction, it may seem like you are reading a fantasy. It seems like a far-fetched reality, but I can tell you it is not a fantasy. It is reality. it is a reality I have lived. Thousands of people are becoming millionaires right here in America every year. Why shouldn't one of those be you?

Ask yourself out loud "Why not me? Why shouldn't I become a millionaire?" The truth is you can! You just have to put in the work, open up your mind to believe it, and you have to develop what I call the "millionaire mindset."

When you see this box, repeat the millionaire affirmation inside.

MILLIONAIRE   AFFIRMATION

"I have a millionaire's mindset."

Sit back and enjoy this book and the journey on which you are about to embark. I will share wisdom that you can apply to your daily life; ideas, principles, and action steps that if implemented, will change your life.

My journey includes the ability to be able to help the needy, pay for my kids' college, my daughter's wedding, and help so many people outside of myself.

I wrote this book to help you be who you were created to be. It is possible for you! It is not a dream. It is a reality. Start peeling off all those labels, all those beliefs about money that do not serve you. I want you to stop tolerating being broke. I want you to stop tolerating just surviving and having too much month left at the end of your money. The buck stops here!

I want you to stop seeing money as a bad thing because it is not. Let's begin this journey with an open heart and an open mind to receive what we are going to learn today.

Thank you for making the best investment that you could ever make; an investment in yourself. I hope and pray that *The Makings of a Millionaire Mind* will be a blessing to you like it has been to my clients.

I want you to know one last thing. You are worthy and deserving of God's best!

Part 1

Becoming a
Millionaire

Chapter 1
Your Money Beliefs

Money. You either love it or you hate it.

Money. You either value it or you don't.

Have you ever asked yourself this question: Where did my relationship with money come from? Think about that for a moment.

There are many factors that contribute to our thought processes about money, how we see money; whether we value money or we don't value money, whether we see it as important or unimportant.

In this part of the book, we are going to dive into how you see money, value money, and consider where your beliefs about money originated. It will be a lot to look into so get ready for the journey. Make sure you have something to write with, a highlighter, and something to write on. Remember, writing things down will help you retain the information.

Let's go a little bit deeper. Where did your beliefs about money come from? Do you believe that money is the root of all evil? Do you believe that rich people are greedy? These are questions that I want you to consider because we all have false beliefs about money. The reality is that the belief systems that we have regarding money were inherited, often from our parents or close relatives.

I am 48 years old. Growing up during the Great Depression, my grandfather's relationship with money was affected by scarcity and lack. Deep thought patterns were formed about money. That affected how my parents felt about and treated money. It affected every financial decision they made, from the restaurants they frequented, the department stores where they shopped, to the vehicles they purchased.

Grab your pen and paper. I want you to draw a T bar at the top of your page. On one side, write down your positive beliefs about money. On the other, write out some of the negative beliefs that you hold about money. Do you believe money is the root of all evil? Do you believe rich people are greedy? Do you often say "I can't afford that, it's too expensive?"

Which belief about money surprised you the most?

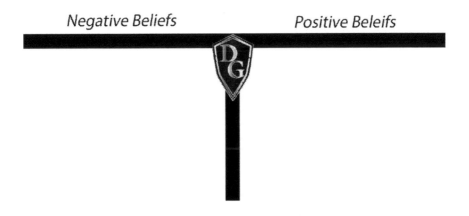

Before you become a millionaire, you have to start thinking like a millionaire. Before you become a multi-millionaire you have to start thinking like a multi-millionaire. You don't become a millionaire before you start thinking like one. That's not the way it works. You have to inherit the thought processes, the mindset... *The Makings of a Millionaire Mind.*

> *Before you become a millionaire, you have to start thinking like a millionaire.*

What are the makings of a millionaire mind? There are several key ingredients. Let's start by reframing your subconscious and cognitive thinking processes. 95% of our habits are subconscious. We do not even realize we do them! We're not even aware of 95% of the things we do every single day. We do these things out of habit and ritual.

When you take a shower, do you wash your head first? Or do you wash your body first? Do you think about changing your routine? For most of us, the answer is no. We are not even aware of what we are doing, we are getting clean, so why change it?

> *You are going to have to go deeper to find the root of your money problems.*

That is exactly how most of us relate to money. 95% of how we use our money is a habit and we are not even aware of it. We just do it automatically.

If you are having money problems, those problems are just a symptom of a root cause. You are going to have to go deeper to find that root. Many people want to place a band-aid on the symptom instead of dealing with the real issue. It's time we start dealing with the cause of it.

What are some beliefs you have about money? Do you believe that you have to work hard, that you have to be a liar and a cheater in order to become successful? Do you believe that you cannot have a balanced life if you want to be wealthy? Do you believe that the rich just get richer and the poor just get poorer? What are some of your beliefs that are holding you back?

Do you believe that life is hard if you have a lot of money? Do you believe that wealthy people are selfish? Do you believe that rich people lie? Do you believe that rich people are stingy? What belief do you have that is keeping you from considering that being wealthy is possible for you?

Here is the truth. It is possible!

Using the *Makings of a Millionaire Mind* principles, that you can make something of yourself! I am going to introduce you to some millionaire affirmations that I encourage you to put into practice. Say them every day, write them in your notes, on your bathroom mirror, etc. You have to get intentional about becoming a millionaire.

The work that I have done on myself in past years has been done very intentionally. My wife thought I was crazy when I was writing 30 or 40 of these affirmations all over our brand-new glass mirror in our new dream home. Sometimes you have to be a little bit crazy. You have to be crazy enough to believe in your own dream and if your dream is to become a millionaire, you have to do things that other people are not willing to do. Sometimes that looks a little crazy.

As you repeat the millionaire affirmations, I want you to receive them for yourself. Once you receive them, then I want you to believe them. As you embrace these affirmations, you will start to believe "Maybe this is possible." As you embody these millionaire affirmations, you will begin to attract new people and new opportunities into your life because you are now living life at a higher frequency, a new level.

I am reminded of one of my clients, Reggie. Reggie and I often worked out together at our gym. The more we hung out together the more his mindset shifted. Within 3 months, Reggie was attracting higher paying clients. He began valuing himself more. The more he repeated the affirmations the more he realized his life was improving.

 Write down the sentence:
I must be INTENTIONAL.

I want you to capitalize INTENTIONAL. Write that down right now in your notebook. I know I am putting you to work early in this book, but I am going to challenge you to stretch yourself throughout this book.

I want you to expand your thinking, stretch your mind, stretch your spirit. A stretched mind and a stretched belief system cannot retract to its original size. I want you to know that being wealthy is possible for you.

I grew up on the south side of San Antonio, Texas. One of the beliefs I had to overcome was "I can't afford that." I remember going into a department store called *Shoppers World* when I was a kid. I would tell my mom I wanted a new pair of sneakers and her response was "We can't afford it." Actually, it didn't matter what it was that I asked for, that was always her response. It was automatic.

I challenge you, from this day forward, instead of saying "I can't afford it," start changing the narrative and ask yourself "How can I afford this?" This will create a shift in your thought patterns leading to a shift in your mindset and ultimately lead to a radical change in your relationship with money, developing your millionaire mindset.

Other false beliefs that people have about money: "When I become wealthy, everyone will want to borrow money from me. I'll have to hide!" "Money doesn't make you happy." Most people that say "Money doesn't make you happy" have never had enough money to test this theory. They say it because it helps to justify the fact that they are always broke.

According to a Federal Reserve Survey conducted in 2019, almost 40% of American adults wouldn't be able to cover a $400 emergency with cash, savings or a credit-card charge that they could quickly pay off. According to data compiled by Nielsen, the American Payroll Association, CareerBuilder, and the NEFE, between 50 percent and 78 percent of employees earn just enough to pay their bills each month, classifying them as living paycheck to paycheck.

The Makings of a Millionaire Mind was written to help develop in you the mindset to become a millionaire!

I do not want you to be a statistic like that anymore. I want your life to change from this day forward. Did you pay attention to what you just read? Most people do not have enough money in their savings to cover a small emergency like a doctor's visit or a simple car repair, etc. Are you living paycheck-to-paycheck?

As we go forward, I encourage you to be INTENTIONAL. *The Makings of a Millionaire Mind* was written to help develop in you the mindset to become a millionaire!

REFLECTION CHECK POINT

1. Where did your relationship with money come from?

2. What false belief about money do you need to let go of?

3. On a scale of 1-10, how committed are you to being intentional?

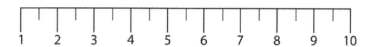

CHAPTER 2
THE MONEY SHIFT

Now I am going to give you some new beliefs about money. We are going to override the conditioning that has been hardwired in your subconscious mind. Let's start talking about some new belief systems that can help you build the next level of success and wealth in your life and business.

You might be saying "Daniel, is this obtainable?" Can I really become a millionaire? Can I really achieve this level of success, the millionaire lifestyle?

Yes, you can! If I can do it, you can do it. I am no better than you. I have put in the work and just by you picking up this book, I know you are ready to do the work. It is not going to be easy, but anything worth accomplishing never is. You have to be committed and want it for yourself.

Here are the first new beliefs I want you to have about money: Money gives you freedom! Money allows you to contribute to and help people. One of the greatest gifts that my wife and I have experienced is the ability to help thousands of homeless and needy people by contributing to and improving their lives. By giving to the SAMMS Ministry here in San Antonio, we have helped house, feed and clothe people when they were at their lowest. It is a reward like no other.

There are moments when I'm feeling down and not having a great day. I wish I had a perfect day every day, but the reality is that even Daniel Gomez does not have a great day every single day. Whenever I find myself at less than 100%, I like to go find a way I can give and support somebody. You need money to be able to help people in this way. Money allows you to be generous. Money allows you to show compassion in a way you couldn't without it.

Money gives you the freedom of having options.

Money gives you the freedom of having options. You have the freedom to do what you want to do. You have a choice to further your education. I would never have been able to send my kids to college. My daughter, Alicia, just graduated from the University of San Antonio with her MBA in Architecture. If you had told me 10 years ago that I was going to be paying $100,000 for a college education without going into debt, I would have never believed it. I remember getting my acceptance letter to the University of Texas in Austin, I was so excited! The unfortunate reality was that my dad couldn't afford to send me to college. The more I think about it, we didn't have the belief that anyone in our family could get a degree.

My son Julian, is graduating from Texas State next year with a BA in music. I am grateful that both of my children get to move forward in their lives without thousands and thousands of dollars of student loan debt hanging over their heads. Money allows you the choice of furthering your education.

Let's start erasing the negative belief systems you have about money and start reprogramming your mind with new, positive ones. Let's start building your millionaire mind.

I want you to receive it. Believe it. Embrace it for yourself. Embrace it for your family. Embody it. Embody the new identity of being a millionaire!

Money allows you to enjoy life! It allows you to go on vacations. Do you know how many people cannot afford to take a week off and really enjoy it? Imagine being able to go on vacation and not worry at all about the money you are spending.

Recently we took a vacation with some friends. Let's call them John and Mary. They who were so worried about what they were spending that they could not enjoy themselves. In my mind, you go on vacation to enjoy yourself. But the sad part is, you can't enjoy it if you are too worried about the money that you are spending. John and Mary really didn't get a vacation because of their money concerns.

This is a poor-man's financial inner economy that we need to eliminate from our mindsets. We need to become intentional about developing a millionaire's financial inner economy.

Too many people have a poverty consciousness and deep down, that poverty consciousness keeps them from succeeding and prevents them from developing a prosperity consciousness, a millionaire's financial DNA. This breaks my heart. I believe God created us to prosper and multiply.

Let's change your belief system. Maybe you have been striving for a new career, applying for a new job, but you have a poor self-image of yourself. When you have a poverty consciousness, you have a poor self-image of who you are and of what you can become. You are never going to earn more than what your self-image allows. If you have a poor self-image of yourself, it will prevent you from attracting a high-quality position, living a higher standard of life and keep you from succeeding and becoming all that you were born to be.

According to a Reader's Digest (January 4, 2022) article entitled, "13 Things Lotto Winners Won't Tell You: Life After Winning the Lottery", Michelle Crouch says "Whether they win $500 million or $1 million, about 70% of lotto winners lose or spend all that money in five years or less."

> *"If someone hands you a million dollars, best you become a millionaire, or you won't get to keep the money."*
> *– Jim Rohn*

Do you know why 70% of lottery winners are in worse financial shape five years AFTER winning the lottery? It is because deep within them, they still feel poor. They are holding on to the poor-minded financial inner economy that they inherited from their parents. They don't have the capacity to handle this level of finances or success.

As the great Jim Rohn once said, "If someone hands you a million dollars, best you become a millionaire, or you won't get to keep the money." Just because you have a million dollars in your possession does not make you a millionaire. You have to develop a millionaire mindset, the character, and the foundation. You probably know someone who was an "overnight success" that soon lost it all. They didn't have the millionaire's financial inner economy to support that level of success.

As you raise your self-image, you raise the things that you attract to yourself and raise your income. Ask yourself, "What can I do to shift from a poor man's financial inner economy to a rich man's financial inner economy so I can envision myself succeeding and becoming a millionaire? "

One of *The Makings of a Millionaire Mind* is a millionaire's financial inner economy. I remember when God blessed us with our new home. As we were moving in, I found clothes in my closet that I had owned for several years but had never worn. I tried to convince myself that I needed to keep these clothes because I would wear them one day soon. I had a hard time letting go of these clothes because I was letting go of the old idea of who I was.

I used to be an avid motorcycle rider and I had some apparel from a popular motorcycle brand. These clothes were linked to my old identity, my old self-image. That self-image did not serve me anymore. That's not who Daniel Gomez wanted to be. It was part of my transition from my old identity to my new identity of "I am the million-dollar man, Daniel Gomez Inspires."

It could start as simple as changing the way you dress. Take action now and get rid of the clothes that you have not worn in a while. Those outfits are not who you are any longer. It took me some time to work through this step but now when I dress, I dress as the person I want to become. I feel better because I dress better. I am not saying you have to go out and buy an expensive suit. I, myself, do not wear suits as much as I used to. Dress nice and sharp, whatever that is for you, and you will feel better about yourself. It's time to RAISE your self-image and soar!

 Write this question down in your journal: What can I do to raise my self-image, to see myself as more so that I can be more, have more and do more?

The truth is you were born to make millions. You were born to have a rich man's financial DNA, to be prosperous. Maybe a poor self-image is the one thing that is holding you back.

When you grow your self-image, your bank account will grow. It's amazing how when you elevate one part of your life, other areas of your life automatically follow suit.

I want you to write this millionaire affirmation on your mirror:
I have a Millionaires Self-Image.

You have to see yourself as a millionaire. Walk like a millionaire, talk like a millionaire and be that millionaire. This is all part of possessing a rich man's financial inner economy. Start envisioning yourself as a millionaire. You may not believe it right away, but with some intentional work over time, it will happen. I could see that I was becoming this new, successful, millionaire, Daniel Gomez. It was happening right before my eyes.

This process is going to be painful as you put forth the effort to rid yourself of the poor-minded financial inner economy. That is not who you are anymore. It is not part of your identity. Let me remind you, you picked this book up for a reason. I truly believe that reason was so you can become a different person after reading it. God did not create you to be poor. God did not create you to just get by. God created you to life a limitless life. He created you to be a blessing to the people around you.

I challenge you to do whatever it takes to go from a poor-minded financial inner economy to a millionaire-minded financial inner economy and develop a millionaire mind.

REFLECTION CHECK POINT

1. Do you feel like you can enjoy money?

2. What freedom are you looking forward to having when you have plenty of money?

3. What was your biggest takeaway from this chapter?

CHAPTER 3
MORNING ROUTINE

How do you go from a poor man's financial DNA to a millionaire's financial DNA? How do you go from having a poor-minded financial inner economy to a millionaire's financial inner economy? How do you go from one extreme to the other?

 You need to be intentional. Write this word in your notebook:

INTENTIONAL

Remember to take notes as if you will be teaching this information. Writing truths down will help you retain the knowledge within these pages.

You have to be intentional in everything that you do on a daily basis. One step towards becoming more intentional starts with putting together a morning routine. This will help you develop new beliefs and new prosperity consciousness.

Maybe you do not have a morning routine in place already. Maybe you are thinking "Daniel, I have never had a morning routine." You might be one that rises out of bed, splashes water on your face, prepares your coffee and gets dressed without being intentional before going about your day. A good morning routine will help set your day up for success. This does not happen by accident. It takes deliberate steps to be intentional.

The key to changing belief systems and embracing new ideas about money and success is in the power of the morning routine. Here is an example. Let's say, you have to be at work at 8:30 a.m. If you know you can leave your house at 8:00 a.m. and arrive just in time for work, you might be tempted to wake up at 7:45 a.m., rush to get ready, rush to get out of the house, fight through traffic and, of course, everything that could go wrong does go wrong. Why is that?

The key to changing belief systems and embracing new ideas about money and success is in the power of the morning routine.

You have put yourself in a rush mentality. You pull up to a red traffic light and the next thing you know you are being impatient, and anxiety builds up. You did not set your morning up for success. You set yourself up for being anxious and frustrated all day by putting extra pressure on yourself. Your morning routine has the power to set the tone for the rest of your day. But you have to be intentional.

When I realized that I could control how my day went just by developing a healthy morning routine, it was a game-changer. I now had the power to set my day up for success.

When you have victory in the morning, everything changes. What are the aspects to my healthy morning routine? Well, I am glad you asked!

My morning schedule starts with waking up at 4 a.m. I spend the first 15 minutes of my day repeating millionaire affirmations. This may sound crazy to you but let me ask you, how bad do you want results? Do you want to go from the poor man's financial inner economy to a millionaire's financial inner economy? How hungry are you to become successful? When are you going to get tired of being tired? When are you going to be fed up with always being broke? When are you going to get frustrated with always being poor and not having enough? Are you tired of having a lean wallet, yet?

I'll never forget when we moved into our dream house a couple of years ago. My wife thought I was crazy, but that is okay. She thinks a lot of things I do are crazy. We each have our own mirror in the bathroom. I filled mine up with 35 millionaire affirmations about success and money. Yes, you read that right, 35 affirmations written out on my bathroom mirror.

Why do I say these affirmations first thing in the morning? When we wake up in the morning, our mind and body are still in the theta stage of sleep. This is the time when our minds are most programmable, as we are coming out of that dream state. This is why it is important to be deliberate and intentional first thing in the morning.

Poor-minded, average people wake up and grab their nearby phones to answer emails and texts, or to browse social media before our feet ever hit the ground. That is the worst thing you can do! We may see a post online that upsets us, or causes us to be jealous or frustrated. We may get a concerning email that we feel like needs to be taken care of immediately. We may lose track of time browsing social media, making us late in getting ready for the day. We have just set the mood for the day before we ever get out of bed. I know because this was me. These were habits that I had to change in order to build that millionaire mind. I had to develop my millionaire habits. It took work, a lot of work!

A main key to reframing your cognitive thinking is repetition.

From this day forward, I challenge you to remove your phone from your bedside or under your pillow. The last thing you want to do is set yourself up for failure first thing in your day. Moving your phone out of your bedroom will help you avoid negativity as part of your morning routine. Charge your phone in another room and set yourself up to succeed and develop your millionaire mind. Don't let anything come between you and that bathroom mirror full of millionaire affirmations!

One of the main keys to reframing your cognitive thinking is repetition. Listen, the main thing that is going to help you go from a poverty consciousness to a prosperity consciousness, millionaire mind, is repetition. By being intentional about what you wake up to every morning; "Money comes to me easily and freely," "Money flows to me," "I am receiving miracle money every day," "All of the money that I circulate returns to me multiplied in a never-ending cycle of increase and enjoyment," "I am attracting millions every day," "I was born to make millions," "I declare millions of dollars are flowing into my bank accounts," "It is easy to make money." All of these affirmations are part of my daily morning routine and have been the catalyst to transformation in my life.

After 15 minutes of repeating millionaire affirmations in my mirror, I move my focus to my vision board. This may sound even crazier to you but remember, I told you I was intentional and sometimes intentional looks a little bit crazy!

We have our vision boards over our toilet.

No, not everyone can see them when they come to our house.
They are tucked away. But I look at our vision boards every
single morning after saying my millionaire affirmations. These
are the first pictures I see. Millionaires understand that the
pictures that they take in on a daily basis affect the way they
think.

 Write this down in your notebook:
The dominant pictures in your head pull
you
toward your future.

What better pictures to see each morning than those on your
vision board? Soak them in!

I remember when we purchased this dream house that we are
now living in. So many of the details that we wanted in a
house were first dreamt about on my vision board. It was
amazing to look back at how many of those details were first
part of my vision. For months and months before moving
here, we would visualize that vision board and feel the
gratitude, feel the happiness, feel the joy of getting our new
dream home.

Details on mine and my wife's vision board were amazing
down to the horseshoe driveway and the lights around the
house. These details were part of the dominant pictures that
we put in our minds every day.

Let me ask you, what pictures are you taking in daily? What
are you looking at first thing in the morning?

After I am done soaking in the images on my vision board, I
spend 45 minutes to an hour in prayer. I include in this time

reading positive words of wisdom and then meditating on those words. I give myself that time to let the wisdom soak in and fill me up spiritually in God's presence.

After my prayer time, I will read, listen to an audio, or watch a video for 10 to 15 minutes, followed by an hour of working out.

This is a short yet powerful and effective morning routine that if you implement it into your life and you are intentional every morning, even on weekends, can change your life.

Be consistent and allow yourself to develop the habit of a healthy morning routine.

Here is an example of my morning routine:

4:00 - 4:15 Millionaire affirmations
4:15 - 4:20 Soak up Vision board
4:20 - 5:15 Prayer time, reading, spending time with God, meditating
5:15 - 5:30 Reading something positive (sometimes hypnosis)
6:00 - 7:00 Workout time

I get all of this done in 3 hours each morning. This morning routine is what has helped me to accelerate the results I have gotten in my life in order to live the life that we are living now.

Many people start this journey of changing their lives, really wanting better for themselves, but the sad part is that they want to see instant results. And when they don't get instant gratification, they give up. In order for your life to change, you must change your habits.

I want you to write this word down:
COMMIT.

I want you to commit to yourself right now. You cannot merely be interested in becoming a millionaire. It takes commitment. There is a huge difference between being interested and being committed. People who are interested in developing a prosperity consciousness, interested in success, interested in building wealth; they are only going to do what is convenient. They are going to take the easy path. Once adversity comes, they give up. They quit.

We all have that friend or family member who is always trying something new, jumping from interest to interest. They cannot stick to anything because they are hopping from idea to idea. When you make a commitment, you do whatever it takes to succeed.

Living the millionaire life takes commitment. You have to do the things that you don't want to do in order to go to the next level. You have to go through times of frustration and seasons of character building. Those seasons will make you stronger and are expanding and stretching your mind and heart. They are expanding your belief system to believe and receive more!

I don't want you to merely be interested in becoming a millionaire, I want you to be committed.

MILLIONAIRE AFFIRMATIONS

"I am committed to being a millionaire.
I am committed to making millions.
I am committed to becoming a millionaire."

Make that commitment to yourself right now. That's you, committed!

When you are committed, you put the work in and do the small things that inconvenience you. That's the difference between being interested in being committed. You must be willing to do whatever it takes to become wealthy and prosper.

REFLECTION CHECK POINT

1. What is the worst habit you've developed as part of your morning routine?

2. What part of your routine are you changing starting tomorrow morning?

3. Make the commitment to do the small things that inconvenience you now for the rewards that will come later.

CHAPTER 4
RAISING THE B.A.A.R.

As you are saying your millionaire affirmations, I want you to close your eyes and visualize your desired future.

Take a minute and repeat these affirmations ten times. Don't rush it. Feel it and envision the wonderful things you are going to do by becoming a millionaire. Let it soak in.

MILLIONAIRE AFFIRMATIONS

"I am committed to being a millionaire.
I am committed to my success."

We just covered the importance of a morning routine. Now let us look at an evening routine. Yes, there is an evening routine also!

What does your current evening routine look like right now? Do you have a structure to the end of your day? We are going to specifically focus on the last hour of your day. Many people make the mistake of ending their evening watching TV that doesn't add value to them, watching the news or maybe even watching a scary movie and then wonder why they have negative thoughts when they wake up in the morning.

A Millionaire Mind is intentional about what you are taking in. Trash in equals trash out. This is even more important to remember in the evenings because your subconscious mind absorbs and replays the last things you see before you go to sleep.

From this point forward, I want you to be intentional about the last hour of your day. Cut out the trash TV, turn off the evening news, and remove anything that is not adding value to you. You have to be intentional about this. I have accomplished desired results in my life and business because of the small changes I've made that have paid huge dividends! So, let's go over my evening routine.

I write down five things that are important to me that I want to accomplish the next day. Don't confuse this with a to-do list. Writing these five items down activates your subconscious mind to begin the steps of accomplishing what's important.

 What are 5 activities you need to accomplish? Write them down!

After you write them down, rank them in order of importance from number one to number five. This helps set yourself up for success from the time you wake up each morning. Then read a few pages in a book or listen to a few minutes of an audio that is going to add value to you. You might watch a video of a goal that you have, a place you want to visit, a house you want to own, etc. Spend the last 15 minutes before bed visualizing some of your goals actually coming to fruition.

Remember, before you become a millionaire, you have to think like one. Millionaires are always prepared.

Once you have written those five activities and ranked them in order of importance, set yourself a bedtime. Discipline yourself to go to bed at a consistent time each night.

You might be thinking, "Daniel, is watching the news really going to hurt me?" Yes, yes, it is. Do you want to continue living a mediocre life? Do you want to be poor-minded? Or are you ready to have a millionaire mindset and a prosperity consciousness?

You are worth the investment.

You are worth the effort.

These are the habits that begin this life change.

Remember, it takes 21 days to start forming a habit and 90 days to make it a lifestyle. Give yourself time to develop these new habits. The only way to replace old habits in our lives is to replace them with new millionaire mindset habits.

You are worth the investment. You are worth the effort.

As you implement your new morning routine and this new evening routine, something amazing begins to happen without you being aware of it. You start raising the B.A.A.R. in your life.

B.A.A.R.

B is for Beliefs. Begin to believe what is possible for you!

A is for Attitude. Begin having a millionaire's attitude, that champion attitude! Your attitude will determine how you approach your day. How you approach your day will determine the actions you take.

A is for Action. Change the actions that you take every day and your behavior will begin to change. Take millionaire actions!

R is for Results. You will begin to notice that your results are changing. You will no longer be getting poor-minded results. You are now getting millionaire mindset results! Your new results will affirm your new beliefs.

It's time to raise the B.A.A.R. in your life. It's time to go to another level. Our beliefs drive the attitude of how we approach something. When you have the right belief system, you have a different approach, a different attitude of how you go about that activity and have a different attitude about what you are doing.

If you have a different attitude, you are going to take different actions. You are going to be more intentional. You are going to take action with expectations. When you start taking this massive action on a daily basis, your results are going to change. As you see your results change, it will validate your new beliefs, your millionaire mindset.

Once you start seeing the new results and that your new belief system is being validated, it strengthens your attitude and approach and gives you more confidence to continue. It is possible for you! Your beliefs feed how you approach your attitude for the day. When you have a millionaire mindset attitude, it changes your actions and behaviors throughout the day. As you begin taking millionaire actions, you start getting millionaire results. Then when you reflect and see the results, it validates that you are making the right choices and you are right on track.

From this day forward, close your eyes and visualize your desired outcome as a millionaire and say it ten times.

M I L L I O N A I R E   A F F I R M A T I O N

"I am raising the B.A.A.R. in my life."

This is your season.

Your time is now!

No one said that becoming a millionaire was going to be easy. It takes work. It takes effort. It takes intentionality. Believe me, I know. There were many times that I wanted to give up but I am glad I didn't.

You would not be reading this book right now had I quit. When you are intentional about your morning routine and you are intentional about your evening routine, you are going to see that B.A.A.R. raise in your life. It is inevitable.

REFLECTION CHECK POINT

1. Do you believe that being a millionaire is possible for you?

2. What millionaire action will you take today to raise the B.A.A.R. in your life?

3. Write down your morning routine for tomorrow.

CHAPTER 5
WORTHY AND DESERVING

There are two factors that prevent us from attracting success, wealth, and our dream life.

1. Feeling Unworthy
2. Feeling Undeserving

Let's dive deep into these two factors. Right now, get out your pen and paper and write down the answer to these questions: What are the lies that you have been believing? What labels have people put on you that make you feel unworthy and undeserving?

Think about your answer. The results you have been getting in life have been because of these labels. Ask yourself, "Where in my life do I feel unworthy? Where in my life do I feel undeserving?" Right down your answer.

Maybe you feel unworthy because you feel you have failed as a parent, as a mom, or as a father. Maybe you feel unworthy because you had an affair and cheated on your spouse. Maybe you are reading this book right now and this question is hitting you and the depths of your soul. Do you hear yourself saying "Daniel, every time I get some wins, whether big or small, and I begin gaining some momentum, I always seem to self-sabotage"?

You are self-sabotaging because you feel unworthy and undeserving. You've been dealing with failure. You have never released the guilt and the shame or forgiven yourself. Remember when I said earlier in this book "We'll either have a poor-minded financial inner economy or we have a millionaire financial inner economy?" Which is your financial inner economy?

Your financial inner economy is what is going to dictate the successes that you are going to have in life. It is going to dictate how far you go in life, and how much wealth and success you have. It does not matter how skilled you are, how many books you read, how many courses you buy, or seminars you go to. Until you change that financial inner economy in yourself, the likelihood is that you will get the same results that you have been getting over and over.

The goal of reading this book is to change your poverty financial inner economy to a prosperous financial inner economy. I call it the millionaire's financial inner economy - that's the goal.

You need to change that inner economy within yourself. Guilt and shame keep us in a poor-minded financial inner economy.

What else is slowing you down? Maybe you got fired from a job and you feel like a failure. Maybe you have some regrets. Did you have an opportunity that you didn't grab? An action in your life that you missed taking? Living with regrets, you are saying "I should have." What if you had taken that job? What if you had started that business? All of these things can leave you feeling unworthy and undeserving of millions.

Don't rush through this process. I feel like some things are going to be revealed to you right now, like God is going to show you what has been keeping you from success.

Maybe you were the child who was told that you could never do anything right, that you were never going to amount to anything. Maybe this has left you feeling unworthy and undeserving. Do you feel like you always mess up? I want you to know that I, myself, have had many failures and many setbacks that have brought me down in my lifetime. I realize that all the mistakes, all the regrets that I had did not define who I was. I was embodying this false identity. When I removed all of the labels that had been put on me, things began to change.

I will never forget a moment along my journey when I was in a parking lot listening to a podcast. I was feeling frustrated that day. I could not figure out what was keeping me from breaking into this millionaire success level. There was a part of me that didn't think that I was deserving, I didn't think I was smart enough to live life as a millionaire.

Imagine that. I, Daniel Gomez, did not believe I was smart enough to be a millionaire and therefore I did not deserve it.

 Take a moment and write down in your notebook what is keeping you from feeling and knowing that you are truly worthy and deserving of millions.

Maybe you wrote down that it was words that your parents have told you that make you believe that you are not worthy or deserving. Maybe it's your ex-spouse that called you a loser, a quitter. Those words have penetrated your heart and soul and have broken you.

One of the lies that we have been told since we were kids on the playground is "Sticks and stones may break my bones, but words will never hurt me." That is so far from the truth. Words stay with us. If you get a cut on your elbow or if you scrape your knee, those wounds will heal over time. But so many times, we carry the words spoken to us for our entire lives. These words can keep us feeling truly unworthy and undeserving of what God wants to give us.

Do yourself a favor right now. This is called a forgiveness exercise. Close your eyes. Think about the root cause that's making you feel unworthy and undeserving. Take a moment and truly forgive yourself, forgive the person who has caused these feelings.

The gift of forgiveness that I gave myself set me free.

Let me walk you through it.

When I went through it, I said "Daniel, I forgive you for not being the father and husband you should have been for many years. I set you free this day, Daniel. You are free to go. I release you this day."

Then say "Jesus, forgive me for not forgiving myself and putting myself above you. Come into my heart even more and help me."

That's it. That is how simple it is to forgive yourself. Or maybe you put someone else's name in there and you forgive them. This is a powerful exercise in forgiveness.

This gift of forgiveness that I gave to myself set me free. When I did this several years ago, it brought freedom and removed a weight from my shoulders. I knew that I was worthy. I knew that I was deserving of becoming a millionaire. It was like the glass ceiling that had been keeping me at that financial status had finally been broken. It was then that I began to build that millionaire financial inner economy within myself.

The truth is that your financial inner economy is going to trump your skill set and your knowledge. You can have all the knowledge that you want, you can have all the skills you can develop, attend every seminar and conference but if you are poor-minded in your financial inner economy, that mindset will trump everything and you will continue to get the same results, living paycheck to paycheck. It's time to give up having more month left at the end of your money.

It is time to build that millionaire financial inner economy, that prosperous financial inner economy within yourself.

I want you to close your eyes and visualize the life you want, the business that you want.

M I L L I O N A I R E   A F F I R M A T I O N

"I am worthy and deserving of being a millionaire."

Visualize all the good that you are going to do with your millions.

I truly believe that this millionaire affirmation will set you free.

REFLECTION CHECK POINT

1. What makes you feel unworthy of God's best for you?

2. Who do you need to forgive? Is it yourself or someone else?

CHAPTER 6
ENVISION YOUR BANK ACCOUNT

As you start believing that you are worthy and deserving of being a millionaire, something amazing happens. It unlocks your belief system. I want you to start believing this for yourself. As you are continuing through this book and taking notes, do the exercises and take action! Remember to be reading this book as if you were going to teach it.

Many of us may pick up a book and read it but we neglect to apply the knowledge gained. Nothing is worse than knowledge that sits dormant within us. There are people around us that need the knowledge we have obtained. What good is knowledge if it is not applied? What good is knowledge if we don't share it?

Think about what you have learned so far in this book and start taking action in your everyday life and in your business.

Let's do this exercise together. Close your eyes and envision your bank account with large numbers. Envision your bank account thriving. Take a minute right now, go online and print out a bank statement. You might have $5 in your account or $500 in your account. You might be one of the few who have $1,000 in your account. Stretch your belief system and expand your mind to see that bank statement with large numbers.

I will never forget when I did this exercise. I wrote down precisely $1,038,978. As I would visualize my bank account growing to this number, I cannot really explain what happened, but I started believing it more and more. I started attracting more clients and our business grew. More opportunities came our way. Doors opened. Paths appeared and bigger and bigger opportunities flowed to me every day.

So, get your white-out and cover over the balance that you currently have on that printed bank statement. Challenge yourself and write a bigger number. It's time you get fed up with having a lean wallet. It's time you get tired of having a lean bank account. It's time to have a full wallet, a full bank account! There is nothing wrong with that. Stop listening to the little voice in your head saying, rich people are greedy and wicked!

Visualize your wallet being full. The days of having a lean bank account are over. Doesn't that give you a sense of peace and freedom?

Are you tired of being broke? You have to be intentional in building that full wallet. I told you that "intentional" is a keyword throughout this book. The days of just getting by are over. The days of just making do are over. This is a new season. Your time is now!

Say these millionaire affirmations right now with me. Close your eyes. Visualize and feel the desired balance you want in your bank account and repeat this:

MILLIONAIRE AFFIRMATIONS

"My time is now to have a full bank account.
My time is now to have a full wallet.
My time is now to have a full purse.
I have millions in the bank."

Visualize how you are going to help those in need. Think about how you will be able to help your family. Think of all the good you can do as you see those numbers on your bank statement increase. Embrace this feeling of joy! Embrace the feeling of freedom to go to the grocery store and not worry about the food you are purchasing. Not having to look at prices before you buy what you really want.

The days of scarcity are over.
The days of lack are over.
The days of not having enough are over.

Your wallet is going from a lean wallet to a full wallet. Your bank account is going from a lean bank account to a full bank account. Doesn't that feel amazing?!?

You have more than enough to give. There is an endless supply of money for all of us.

I want you to start carrying five $100 bills. When I began doing this many years ago, I started attracting more $100 bills. Then I asked my wife to do it. She hid hers towards the back of her purse. I said "No, honey! The whole point of carrying $500 with you in your purse is so that when you open it, you see that money. Don't fold them and hide them in the back."

The peace of mind that comes with carrying five $100 bills with you is indescribable. The point of carrying that much money is not necessarily to spend it. It's to help you attract more of it. If God puts it on your heart to bless someone with $100, it's okay! You have the cash right there to impact someone's life unexpectedly.

Maybe you don't have $500. Start with one $100 bill and work your way up. When you make it your new normal, you are shifting your way of thinking. You are expanding your capacity to receive more. You are going to attract more $100 bills.

The season of having a lean wallet and a lean bank account is over. You are beginning a new season of abundance that includes a full wallet and bank account! It's time to stop settling for the status quo. That is not who you are anymore. God didn't create you to be average! Remember, you are born to make millions.

REFLECTION CHECK POINT

1. What number are you going to write down for your bank balance?

2. Write down the precise date and time you will begin carrying $100 bills around with you.

3. Who will you bless with one of those $100 bills?

CHAPTER 7
MILLIONAIRES
TRUST THE PROCESS

Millionaires don't just read for the sake of reading. They read in order to put their new knowledge into action. They apply their knowledge to their everyday life and their business. This knowledge helps you to grow who you are. Before you can become richer in the physical world, before you manifest that millionaire lifestyle that you want in the outer world, you have to become richer within yourself.

That is exactly what you are doing right now, by reading this book you are becoming richer within yourself. Continue to invest in yourself and don't let knowledge lay dormant. I highly recommend you invest in our online course to help you accelerate your results, *The Makings of a Millionaire Mind* Course at WWW.THEMAKINGSOFAMILLIONAIREMIND.COM.

Millionaires live their new knowledge every single day. As you grow in knowledge, you begin to change your financial inner economy. Your financial inner economy trumps your skill set.

You have to shift your mind and go deep within your reservoirs. As you do this, you shift from having a poverty consciousness to having a prosperous consciousness. You go from a poor-minded financial inner economy to a millionaire's financial inner economy.

Zig Ziglar said, "You don't have to be great to start, but you do have to start to be great." This is going to be a process that you are going to go through. It is not going to be easy. There are going to be days that you will be frustrated. There will be days that you are saying "This is not working!" There are going to be days that you say "Daniel, forget this!"

Remember, that is not you!

You do not want to be part of the status quo anymore. You want to change your life. You want to improve your life. We all start somewhere. As you are going on this journey, don't beat yourself up.

> *You do not have to be part of the status quo anymore.*

Trust the process and know that as you continue to do these activities on a daily basis, as you say your affirmations, you will start seeing this shift in your financial inner economy from that poor-minded financial inner economy to that abundance, prosperous, millionaire's financial inner economy.

Before you know it, you will begin to see the fruit of your work. Remember, before you can become wealthy in the physical world you have to become wealthy within yourself.

When you focus on having a fat wallet, your wallet gets fatter. We always get more of what we focus on. What we focus on expands. What we focus on, we attract. What we focus on, comes to us! Before you know it, as your financial inner economy changes, you're going to start attracting these things so fast. You no longer have to go out there and chase anything down. Opportunities are going to come to you. New doorways are going to open. You are going to see paths clearer than you did before. Big money opportunities are going to come to you continuously. You won't have to chase things as you did before because opportunities will come knocking on your door. Customers will come knocking on your door!

Do the work on yourself, for yourself so that you may help yourself, help your family and help all the people around you. Get comfortable with carrying money around. Those five $100 bills are great to get you comfortable carrying cash. The more you get comfortable carrying cash, the more you see it and visualize it and the more you will attract it to yourself. What you focus on expands.

As you start to see the fruits of your labor, you will feel better about yourself. As I said earlier in this book, your beliefs start to change which means the results that you get are going to change because you start to feel better about yourself. As you feel better about yourself, the results are getting better, right? Your beliefs create the attitude, create the approach and you start raising the bar in your life. When you feel better about yourself your beliefs change.

Maybe you are reading this book and have made a commitment to getting healthier. Maybe you're eating healthier and working out on a more consistent basis. You are not going to see the results from one day to the next. You don't go to McDonald's and eat junk food today, then eat a salad tomorrow and expect to be healthier instantly. Results don't show up in one day. It takes time. You don't go to the gym and run on the treadmill for five or six hours and obtain the body you desire after one workout.

REFLECTION CHECK POINT

1. What are you doing to invest in yourself?

2. What we focus on expands. What will you focus on today?

Chapter 8
You are in a Class of Your Own

When you change the way you view things, things change. It sounds simple, doesn't it?

Millionaires get to the point where they finally realize that they have no need to compare themselves. I remember struggling with this internally. Remember me saying earlier in this book that we'll never grow bigger than our self-image? All these insecurities we have affect our finances. It's who we are. And because of this mindset, I would always compare myself to other people. Keep in mind, I was not doing this deliberately. It was just the self-image that I had formed about myself.

When you realize that you are in a class of your own and that there is no need to compare, there is freedom. There is freedom to grow, to be, do, and have whatever you want!

God told me, "Daniel, you have your own unique classification. You are in a class of your own. There really is no need to compare yourself." For you sports fans out there, it is like comparing the Dallas Cowboys, a professional football team, to a high school football team. Although they are the same sport, they are in completely different classes of football.

It is like comparing a Rolls-Royce to a fully loaded Toyota Camry. There is no comparison because Rolls-Royce is in a class of its own.

Millionaires understand this. Millionaires understand that when they finally get to that level of success, to become that multi-millionaire, you have to stop comparing yourself. Do you know what happens when you compare yourself? You can't see what is going on underneath the surface. The moment you start comparing yourself, you stop producing the genius in you. You lose your creativity. When you lose the ability to become creative, you lose the ability to produce what it takes to be a millionaire.

Creativity is what takes a person to the next level of success, to be able to become a millionaire. When you are playing the compare game, it kills the creativity within you. When you play the compare game, you are wasting your energy and destroying your creative flow.

You need your creativity to stay on point. When you compare, you are shifting your creative energy, your focus, and your strength to other people or situations outside of yourself.

If you are not careful, that's where you lose the core of who you are, your originality.

 Grab your notebook and write down the answer to this question:
"Where in my life am I comparing myself to someone else?"

Take a moment and read your answer or answers back to yourself when you are done.

For me, a breakthrough came when I realized that there was no need to compare myself. I have my own talents. I have my own strengths. I have my own past. The moment you stop comparing yourself, you see the open doors you should walk through. You are no longer blinded by the disease of comparison. You will finally see the doors that were created specifically for you to walk through. The paths become clearer, and you know which one to take. All the confusion that I had was gone the moment I stopped comparing myself.

I realized I had a unique message that I had for the world as a motivational speaker. I no longer envied other motivational speakers. I had the confidence to walk my own path. I began walking in my God-given authority!

The moment you find your door and open it wide open, walk through it and discover the confidence to walk the unique path that God is showing you. Comparison steals these opportunities.

When I stopped comparing, big money opportunities rapidly came to me daily! Because I was no longer comparing myself to anyone, opportunities came to me, and I no longer had to chase them down. The magnetism within me came to life and it was beautiful.

These are your millionaire affirmations that I want you to repeat to yourself out loud. Close your eyes. Visualize and feel who you want to become. Repeat them to yourself three times slowly.

MILLIONAIRE AFFIRMATIONS

"I am a Rolls Royce."
"I am in a class of my own."
"I am a millionaire."

REFLECTION CHECK POINT

1. Do you struggle with jealousy?

2. In what aspect do you find yourself comparing yourself to others?

3. In what area of your life are you most creative?

CHAPTER 9
VALUE SYSTEM

"I belong with the elite."

Many times, we fail to reach the next level of success because we have a poor-minded financial inner economy. When you start to develop a millionaire's financial inner economy, you will see that you belong with the elite. There is no reason to feel that you do not belong.

When you stop comparing yourself, you realize you belong. Every human being wants a sense of belonging. Every human being has the longing in their heart and soul, to belong, to do more.

As you read this book and take notes, tell yourself "I belong with the elite." Close your eyes and visualize the dream life that you want. Repeat to yourself" I belong with the elite. I belong with the best of the best." Feel yourself belonging!

When you stop comparing yourself, your value system changes. Think about Superman. When he opens his shirt and you see that large S, you know he is something special. All of us have a large "VS" on our chests. It stands for our value system. The decisions that we make daily are impacted by our value system. Our value system is based on how we see ourselves.

For example, on a scale of 1-10, if you value yourself as a level 7, your life will be tapped out at 6. You will never go beyond the level of value of how you see yourself. Many of us have a low value system. I would even go as far as to say most of us are at a 3 or 4 all because of a poor-minded financial inner economy. But that is no longer for you.

I believe it is a realistic goal to grow one or two levels on the scale each year. In order to do that, you have to be intentional. There's that word again! INTENTIONAL. You have to be intentional about doing the work that it takes to grow your value system.

Read this book again once you are finished. Listen to the audio version every day for the next 6 months. This is how intentional you must be because that is where the true transformation is going to happen.

I want to impact you, not just have you read "just another" book. I want your life to change. When you start to read the material in this book and listen to it each day on audio, this is where the transformation begins. This is where the paradigm shifts. I also highly recommend you invest in one of our live seminar workshops to help you accelerate your results even more, *The Makings of a Millionaire Mind* Workshop at WWW.THEMAKINGSOFAMILLIONAIREMIND.COM.

As your value system goes up on the scale of 1 to 10, the dead weight in your life is removed and you go to the next level. You begin to develop the millionaire mindset that's on the upper end of the value system scale.

I want you to take this action step right now.

Stop reading and write down in your notebook what your value system is. Ask yourself "How much do I value myself? What is my value system?"

The quality of our lives is determined by the quality of the questions we ask ourselves. What is your value system? Take a moment and write down your answers.

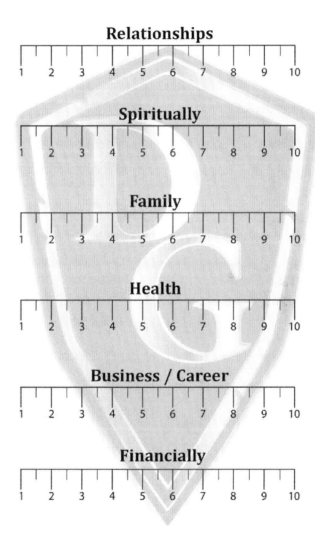

So, what did you write? Where, on a scale of 1 to 10, did you place your value system? What is your overall all value system score for all categories combined? This can help you reveal a blind spot in your life.

On the surface, I thought I valued myself at a level 10. But the more work I did on myself, the more I realized that I was probably a level 5 when I started my journey. I began being intentional 5 years ago in growing and developing who I was, to rid myself of my poor-minded financial inner economy and develop a millionaire's financial inner economy to change my legacy and the lives of my family members.

Remember when you go from level to level, not only does your value system inside of you go up, but you also start making better decisions. Every decision we make depends on how we see ourselves and how much we value ourselves. The truth is, you are more valuable than you realize. God created you. He doesn't make mistakes!

Close your eyes. Visualize and feel yourself becoming more valuable. Repeat them to yourself three times slowly.

Write these millionaire affirmations down and repeat them to yourself out loud.

MILLIONAIRE AFFIRMATIONS

"I am plenty."
Or maybe for a different twist, use your name.
Speak your name and tell yourself you are valuable.
"{Your Name Here} is valuable. I am valuable."

On my journey, these became part of my morning routine. I let these millionaire affirmations sink into my heart and soul, deep down inside. The benefits from saying these millionaire affirmations are amazing! They helped me to realize I truly am invaluable. I am priceless! You are priceless too!

When you are becoming millionaire-minded, it really helps you to make better quality decisions about how you live your life. Having a millionaire mindset is not just about the money, it's about the quality of your whole life, every aspect. You see things from a totally different perspective.

Having a millionaire mindset is not just about the money, it's about the quality of your whole life, every aspect.

The money part is very important. Money allows you to help people. You become more compassionate, more caring, and more loving. Since you are not comparing yourself to anyone else, you see things from a whole different point of view, in a completely different light. A higher value system changes your world!

Like I said before, millionaires are some of the most generous people you will ever meet. I am so grateful that you are on this journey with me. I really want to help you. I want you to be who you were created to be.

REFLECTION CHECK POINT

1. Based on the decisions you have been making, where do you think your value system has been?

2. What was the most surprising area when you evaluated the value system in the different areas of your life?

3. What actions are you going to take to start valuing yourself more?

CHAPTER 10
FINANCIAL THERMOSTAT

As you start to value yourself more, everything in your life is going to rise and everything in your business is going to elevate. When you value yourself more, you raise the setting of your financial thermostat. Yes, you raise the level of your financial thermostat.

When we have our financial thermostat on a low setting, we undervalue who we are. I recently worked with a client whose financial thermostat was set at $40,000. I had asked her what she made over the previous few years. Her answer was approximately $40,000. I challenged her to raise her value system and something amazing happened. The moment she started seeing that she possessed more value, her revenue rose. Her income was not growing every year because she did not value herself the way she should.

She wrote down the words "financial thermostat." I want you to write those same words in your journal. I want you to be honest with yourself and write down where you think your financial thermostat is set.

Millionaires of course have their thermostat set at Millions. When you have your financial thermostat set at millions, you attract millions. You begin to attract the situations and contract opportunities that are now at the next level of business.

You do not become a millionaire and then begin thinking like one. You must first think like a millionaire and then you become one. When you have a millionaire mindset, you set your financial thermostat to millions. This is a level that most of us never fathom reaching. It's not a dream, it is obtainable.

 Now answer this question in your journal: "What is keeping my financial thermostat from rising?"

As you examine the setting on your financial thermostat, you are examining how much you have valued yourself in the past. Wherever your financial thermostat is set at this moment in your life reflects what you have done in the past.

Think about where you want to raise your financial thermostat to. I challenged my client to raise it to $95,522. We chose this odd number because the more detailed the target, the greater the odds that you are going to hit the target. I knew that with her talent level, she could reach this goal. When I put that number out there for her, it stretched her to envision herself making that amount of money. Her business started growing when she decided to raise her financial thermostat.

Many of you reading this book have not made that decision. Make the decision today and make the commitment to raise your financial thermostat. Make it a detailed, specific number. What is that number for you? Maybe you have been teetering and your revenue has been at $150,000. Maybe your new target, your new financial thermostat needs to be set at $300,000.

You must decide today what you are going to raise your financial thermostat to. You must be intentional. There's that word again! If you are not intentional, it is not going to happen by itself.

After my client set her financial thermostat to $95,522, she printed some colorful full-page size printouts with this amount on them and hung them in her office, her bathroom, and around her house. She focused on that number. Remember, what you focus on expands.

Day in and day out, she saw $95,522. I will tell you that she came close to hitting that goal for her revenue because she decided to raise her financial thermostat. She attracted the right people, the right situations, and the right opportunities because of her level of commitment.

> *It's time you go from a poor-minded financial inner economy to a wealthy man's financial inner economy.*

I came from an automotive background, and we always had those top producers in sales. I always wondered why there was always a salesperson that knocked it out of the park every single month, regardless of the time of year. There was one guy who always seemed to make his 20-car sales goal. That's where his financial thermostat was set. The marketplace will pay you what you ask of it.

There were other salespeople that struggled to sell three or four cars. Same receptionist, same dealership, same inventory, same clientele, same demographic, etc. Now, as I go back and work with some of these salespeople, I realize that some of them have their financial thermostat set low. If you have your financial thermostat is set low, you have to ask yourself do I have a poor-minded financial inner economy, or a millionaire minded financial inner economy.

Your financial inner economy is going to dictate your actions and the amount of money you are going to make. It's time you go from a poor-minded financial inner economy to a millionaire-minded financial inner economy. It's time to raise your thermostat!

So how do you raise your financial thermostat internally? I am going to give you four things that I want you to be intentional about to help you raise your financial thermostat, to have the millionaire mindset.

I want to ask you to evaluate four areas of your life.

What are you listening to daily?
What are you watching?
What are you reading?
And what is your environment?

What are you listening to?

Are you listening to music that is not adding value to you on your way to work? I'll never forget, one day a mechanic showed up and was visibly upset. He went to his stall to go work on a vehicle and they gave him his work order. He snapped. No wonder he was upset, he was listening to some heavy metal angry music on his way to work that morning. Not that I have anything against metal music, but this music had an angry theme.

If you are listening to music that angers you, you are probably going to have an angry temperament because that is just a vibration of that music. That music does not add value to you. Maybe you are listening to political radio in the morning, and it causes frustration or anger. Is it adding value to you? No, it is putting you in a negative mindset. Millionaires don't listen to negative news or talk radio. It's useless!

One of the first conferences I ever went to over 20 years ago was with Brian Tracy. Brian challenged us to make our vehicle a university on wheels. He told us about a study that showed that listening to audio material every day for one year is the equivalent of a college education.

Once I heard this, I was hooked. I ended up buying some audio material and I listened to it every day. My mind and my perspective had begun to shift. I started shifting to a millionaire mindset. As a matter of fact, the title of the audio that I had purchased was *21 Secrets of Self-Made Millionaires.*

Commit to adding value to yourself every day.

What are you listening to daily? Commit to adding value to you every day. Maybe listen to our podcast, the "Daniel Gomez Inspires Show." We have valuable content there from amazing people, many of them are millionaires offering priceless gems of wisdom.

Listen to value adding content. Maybe it's an audiobook instead of a podcast. I did not have these resources available when I was growing up. Take advantage of them! It will pay you huge dividends.

What are you watching?

Are you watching the news? Are you watching trash TV? Are you binge-watching Netflix? Is it really serving you? Are you watching scary movies at night before you go to bed? None of these are adding any value to you.

Why not watch something that is going to help you raise your financial thermostat, increase who you are, and add value to you. YouTube is free and full of valuable content if you look for it. Stay away from trash TV and the news!

What are you reading?

Do you know what your life is going to be like in 5 years? Your future is hidden in your daily routine. What you do daily right now is going to be your future in 5 years. I can tell you the person you are going to be in five years by evaluating what you are listening to, what you are watching, what you are reading and looking at your environment.

If you are like me, after I graduated, I had no desire to read a single book. I did not read for many years. I stopped growing. Even though I was successful in many ways, I could have been even more successful had I been intentional about investing in myself.

Even if you are not a book person, I want you to schedule 5 minutes every morning to read something valuable. Incorporate this into your morning routine. Once this becomes a habit, start adding more minutes to the routine.

Remember, it takes 21 days to start forming a habit and 90 days to make it a lifestyle. It's time to build the millionaire lifestyle for yourself.

What is your environment like?

Are you putting yourself in an environment where you are surrounded by people who believe in your millionaire dream? Did you know that your income is within 20% of the average of the five people you spend the most time with?

Back when I was working in the automotive industry, I evaluated the statement and found it to be true. My income was consistent with the five people I spent the most time with. When I made the difficult decision to resign and care for my wife after her breast cancer surgeries, I began surrounding myself with millionaires like Dr. James Dentley and Tony Whatley. My "fab 5" had changed!

Changing the people that I associated with changed my environment. The next thing I knew, I was experiencing new things and my mind began to expand.

Use your highlighter and highlight this statement:

An expanded mind cannot retract back to its original size.

I started experiencing amazing results in business and in life. I began to see things from a different perspective.

Close your eyes and envision the future you want. What will your future look like in 5 years? That dream car, that dream house, that dream vacation, that dream education you want for your kids - that's all going to require a new you, a smarter and more confident you.

By examining these four areas of your life, evaluating what you are listening to, what you are reading and watching, and elevating your associations, you will raise the temperature of your financial thermostat. It will help take you from a poor-minded financial inner economy to a millionaire's financial inner economy. It's time to expect more for yourself! It's time to raise your financial thermostat.

MILLIONAIRE AFFIRMATIONS

"I am elevating my circle of associations.
I am committed to connecting to people that are where
I want to be in life.
I am committed to connecting with higher-level people.
I am committed to connecting with millionaires."

Remember, you are worthy and deserving of success. You are worthy and deserving of God's best. Decide today you are raising your financial thermostat. Go get to work on these four areas.

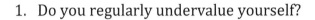

REFLECTION CHECK POINT

1. Do you regularly undervalue yourself?

2. What will you read for 5 minutes tomorrow morning?

3. What will your life look like in 5 years?

CHAPTER 11
BE BOLD ENOUGH TO
INVEST IN YOURSELF

The more I became intentional about what I was listening to, what I was watching, what I was reading, and the environment I was placing myself in, the more I realized that I was investing in the future version of who I was becoming. Many of us often do not focus on investing in ourselves. A great example of that is if someone wants to be an entrepreneur, sometimes they have this false belief that all they have to do is invest in a high-priced course and they will magically become the phenomenal successful entrepreneur with a business. That's not the way it works.

To buy into a McDonald's franchise, you would have to invest over $1,000,000. Before you even make a penny, before you even sell a French fry or Happy Meal, your investment in a McDonald's franchise here in America is well over $1,000,000. Why would someone consider leaving their corporate America 9 am - 5 pm job with no business experience, make a one-time investment, and think they are going to be set for life in business? You have to admit, it sounds too good to be true.

And it is!

Millionaires are comfortable with continuously investing in themselves. The world is changing at a phenomenal pace, especially in this digital era. Things change from year to year, month to month, and even week to week. You have to be innovative. You have to be cutting edge.

Consider our iPhones. We upgrade them almost every year. The same is true for our computers. That is how innovative these electronic products are. If we are going to invest in our electronics, why wouldn't we make the investment in ourselves?

Many of us have an employee mindset. We look at everything considering what it costs. Change your mind set by focusing not on cost, but on investment. You must get comfortable investing in who you are becoming.

Get rid of the myth that a one-time investment in a course or seminar will set you up for success for the rest of your life. I'll be honest with you, if I knew the investment that I was going to have to make in becoming the brand "Daniel Gomez Inspires", "Shield of Faith Coaching", "Sticker Shock Speaking Academy" and now, "The Makings of a Millionaire Mind" book, courses, and seminars I don't know if I would have done it. It can be daunting and overwhelming. I have invested well over $200,000 in our business. I never considered it would take that large of an investment to get us to where we are now.

But on the flip side, those investments are what got us to where we are now! I want to set you up for success in life. Millionaires continue to invest in themselves, day in and day out year after year. Start those millionaire habits now.

Envision the life and business you want. Say these millionaire affirmations "I am a millionaire. I was born to make millions. I am comfortable investing in myself. I am worth the investment."

Let those words soak in. Ladies and gentlemen, you are worth the investment. You are worth the effort. In this era of your life, in this season of your life, you have to get comfortable with investing in yourself. It is a never-ending process. Now I'm not saying to squander and go buy everything that someone tries to offer you. I am saying use wisdom as you examine the areas of weakness in your life and business. Ask yourself "Where do I lack the skills in my life to become the person that I want to become, to achieve the millionaire lifestyle?" Make investments in that area of your life.

> *Being willing to bet on yourself means investing in who you are becoming because the current version of who you are is not going to get you to where you want to go.*

I think about the first time I really invested in myself. I went to a conference in Orlando, Florida just after one of my wife's major surgeries. She had just had her second major surgery after her double mastectomy. It was a trying time in our lives. I could have easily used that as an excuse. Believe me, I was scared to purchase the ticket to the conference! The cost of the ticket was $4,000 plus airfare, meals, and hotel. I had to be willing to bet on me. I had to invest in myself.

If I hadn't been willing to invest in myself, you would not be reading *The Makings of a Millionaire Mind* right now. Millionaires are willing to bet on themselves.

Being willing to bet on yourself means investing in who you are becoming because the current version of who you are is not going to get you to where you want to go.

I remember being at the conference and for the first time in my life, I met an author. I was amazed and excited wondering how awesome it would be to be an author. I remember flying back to San Antonio from Orlando, Florida with an idea planted in my brain. I did not tell anyone about this idea. I started researching steps to becoming an author, then I got nervous. I looked at the costs, and then I got scared. I had second thoughts about becoming an author. But then I began to look at the "costs" as an investment in me.

When I wrote my first book, *You Were Born to Fly,* it was not an easy investment to make. Imagine what I would have missed out on had I not made the investment at that moment in our lives, making a financial investment, to write and publish the book. It became an international bestseller. You Were Born to Fly became the foundation of our 12-Week Mindset Mastery online course and our coaching program. It all came from one book, which has produced thousands in revenue.

Don't be intimidated by what you cannot see. Be bold enough to invest in yourself. The future you is counting on it. I share this story with you because I had every excuse to make. My wife had just had a double mastectomy. I chose not to focus on the excuses and instead to focus on investing in who "Daniel Gomez Inspires" was becoming.

> *Don't be intimidated by what you cannot see. Be bold enough to invest in yourself. The future you is counting on it.*

Because of my investment, you are reading or listening to this book right now. How awesome is that? Have confidence in yourself! Have confidence in your abilities. When you invest in yourself, know you will receive an ROI. Believe it!

This is Daniel Gomez Inspires saying if no one's ever told you they believe in you, I'm telling you right now, I believe in you.

Take action today and bet on you!

REFLECTION CHECK POINT

1. Do you have an employee mindset?

2. How are you boldly investing in yourself today?

3. What's the most amount of money you have invested in yourself?

CHAPTER 12
YOU BELONG
WITH THE ELITE

As you start to invest in yourself, attending conferences and seminars, the more comfortable you will become around successful people. Being around successful people will help you to expand your belief system and grow into who you are becoming. If you keep hanging around small-minded people, you will never have the capacity to handle the next level of success. One thing I want you to understand is millionaires are people just like me and you. We just think differently on a consistent basis. Get comfortable conversing with millionaires.

I say this from experience. I remember back in February of 2020, right before the COVID pandemic happened. We went to the Oscars. We had a dinner planned with Demi Moore. I will never forget what God put in my heart. As the days got closer, I was nervous. God whispered in my ear "Daniel, you belong with the elite." Maybe you need to hear that right now. You belong with the elite. You belong with the best.

We went to the event and had an amazing dinner. I felt like a movie star myself! My wife looked so beautiful! There were some prominent people there. There were some very successful businessmen and women there. In the back of my mind, I kept repeating the phrase that God whispered to me "Daniel, you belong with the elite."

After we heard Demi Moore give her presentation, we had a chance to spend time with her. It was amazing! You have to give yourself permission to play bigger in life. You have to give yourself permission to dream bigger in life. You have to put yourself in rooms with people who are more successful than you.

> *Don't be afraid to put yourself in rooms with people who are wealthier than you.*

Don't be afraid to put yourself in rooms with people who are wealthier than you. At first, you are going to feel like you are not good enough. That is a lie. Do not listen to that lie. It is not the amount of money that is in your bank account that determines who you are. It's who you know that makes you who you are. And you, reading this book, you are a child of God. You are already accepted and loved by God. That's all you need to remember.

You belong in bigger rooms; you belong in bigger events. You deserve to be around these people.

I realized that I could not get to where I wanted to go by myself. Getting comfortable around millionaires and successful people changed my life. You are one idea away, one person away from your next level of success that you want for yourself. One person, one connection! When you realize this truth, you become even more intentional in putting yourself in these bigger rooms and bigger events. When you strike up conversations, you realize these people are no better than you. They love sharing their knowledge. They have a millionaire mindset. What better way to build your millionaire mind than by surrounding yourself with successful millionaires?

I realized from being around some of my great mentors that they are very loving and generous individuals. Some of the best experiences I have ever had growing up in business and entrepreneurship have been because of people like them. You have to give yourself new and bigger experiences frequently.

It's like the old cliche you might have heard. If you are the biggest shark in the tank, it's time you find a bigger tank. Stop being small-minded and know that you belong! You belong with the elite!

MILLIONAIRE AFFIRMATIONS

"I enjoy being in bigger rooms.
I enjoy being around millionaires.
I enjoy being around successful businesspeople."

Close your eyes.

Visualize yourself at a black-tie affair, dressed to the nines, looking stunning with your spouse. I want you to feel your confidence building up as you make your presence known.

The sense of belonging takes over you and you enjoy the evening. You deserve to be at this event.

REFLECTION CHECK POINT

1. When will you schedule your "The Makings of a Millionaire Mind" live event?

2. What "bigger rooms" will you put yourself in over the coming months?

3. Are you the biggest shark in your tank?

CHAPTER 13
KILL YOUR
MIDDLE-CLASS MIND

What is keeping you from connecting with people who have more influence than you? What is keeping you from connecting with millionaires?

One thing that keeps us stuck where we are, is our middle-class minds. Many of us, myself included, have worked so hard to get out of being broke, to stop living paycheck-to-paycheck.

 Grab your journal and write down your answer to these questions: Am I comfortable with my yearly income? Have I gotten too content?

Maybe you have $10,000, $20,000 or $50,000 in your savings account. You might have a chunk of money saved up in your 401K. You might feel like you are doing well for yourself. You might be comfortable. There is that word – comfortable. Nothing is going to kill your destiny, your God-given purpose, like being comfortable.

Many of us middle-class Americans are comfortable. I got stuck there. I remember the first couple of years I made a six-figure income. I thought I had arrived! I had it made. I noticed I began to gain extra weight. I was not taking care of myself. I had gotten lazy. I had plateaued and gotten comfortable with a middle-class mindset. I had stopped dreaming bigger. I got satisfied with my current level of success. This is the worst thing that could have happened to me.

I am going to challenge you today, as we begin the next section of this book, the money files, to kill your middle-class mindset. You have to. You must decide you do not want to be stuck in the middle class any longer. You will not settle for the status quo anymore. It's okay to get to this level of success in your life, but there is more out there for you. Think about this. The more money you make, the more people you will be able to help. The more you will be able to give back to your community.

It's not about you. It's about helping the people around you. You have to develop a positive dissatisfaction with where you are.

It's not about you. It's about helping the people around you. You have to develop a positive dissatisfaction with where you are. What do I mean by positive dissatisfaction? I believe many of us still operate and make decisions based on the beliefs we created as children.: "Just be grateful. Be thankful." And I get it. We definitely need to be grateful because gratitude is the key to more. Having a grateful heart is a key for promotion. I truly believe that.

But I have also seen in my life and in many of our clients' lives that they have a season where they are truly grateful for the level of success they have. But all seasons come to an end. There is a next level of promotion. There is a next level of business, life, and success out there for you. It is okay to have positive dissatisfaction. Never be satisfied. I have said it before, and I will say it again. Some of the greatest rewards I have reaped are in helping the homeless and giving back to women who have been impacted and devastated by breast cancer through our 501c3, the Mari Strong Foundation. It is an amazing feeling that brings joy to my heart. The moment you start living life on the giving side, there is a new sense of fulfillment that cannot be explained until you start living it.

It takes money, it takes wealth to live in generosity and contribute financially. Many of us make it to the middle-class and we are scared to lose it. We stop growing, we stop doing the little things which helped us get there.

I dare you today to kill your middle-class mindset. You have untapped, hidden potential inside of you. You are more capable than you think. You are more capable than you realize. This morning when you woke up, were you satisfied with what you saw in the mirror? Are you satisfied with your current health? Are you in your best physical shape? Be honest with yourself. Is the person in the mirror living life to the fullest?

The sad truth is many of us are not. We make excuses, we settle into a comfort zone, we settle for being content. You might argue, "I don't want to be greedy." It's not about being greedy. It's about going out there and being who you were born to be. It's about challenging yourself to be more, to do more so that you might have more to help more people out there.

As we get ready to enter the money files portion of the book, I want you to decide today, right now, to make a commitment to become a millionaire.

In fact, grab your notebook and write this down and highlight it:
"Today, I am deciding to be a millionaire. I was born for more. Today, I am deciding to be a millionaire!"

Remember the things we declare out loud are 40% more likely to happen. Go find a friend and tell them you have declared that you will be a millionaire. If they make fun of you or belittle your dream, maybe they are not your friend. When you declare or tell someone of your dream to become a millionaire, the likelihood of it happening goes up to 80%.

From this day forward, you are no longer going to settle for the middle class. You are no longer going to settle for being comfortable. You are no longer going to settle for being complacent. Settling is robbing you of your legacy.

You have more in you to give to the world!

I want you to be like a kid and allow yourself to open up your imagination. Allow yourself to think bigger than just being in the middle class. Nothing kills our dreams like complacency.

You are going to feel a level of fear, be a little scared. I get it. I have been there. I tell you; I would not change anything for the world. It has been an amazing ride. I've had the ability to impact thousands so far in my career.

You have more in you to give to the world! I was 44 years old when I left the automotive industry, a job where I was making multiple six-figures, to follow my dream. I'm not going to lie to you, it was scary. I even came up with a quote when I started my career as a professional speaker. "You are not a true entrepreneur until you are in the bathroom crying and you're 99.9% sure you are going to give up. But you don't!"

Close your eyes. I want you to visualize and feel yourself making the decision today that you are going to stop being average. You are not going to merely tolerate your physique anymore. You are not going to allow yourself to settle for being comfortable anymore. God has a purpose for your life. Remember, you are not an accident! You were born for such a time as this.

MILLIONAIRE AFFIRMATIONS

"Today, I am deciding to be a millionaire.
Today, I am deciding to follow my God-given purpose.
Today, I am deciding to live my God-given purpose."

Congratulate yourself for making this powerful decision. I celebrate you because I know it is not an easy decision to make.

I will tell you, the moment I decided to kill my middle-class mind, there was no turning back. Your new life will cost you your old one. Embrace the process. There is another level inside of you and I'm so excited for you. I will see you in the money files.

REFLECTION CHECK POINT

1. What is your current income?

2. How much do you currently have in savings?

3. Are you comfortable?

4. Do you believe you have more to give to the world?

PART 2

THE
MONEY
FILES

THE MONEY FILES
INTRODUCTION

Welcome to the money files, part two of *The Makings of a Millionaire Mind.*

In this part of the book, we are going to find out how millionaires think. We are going to distinguish the difference between how millionaires think compared to poor-minded and middle-class individuals.

 It's time to grab your notebook and take notes. There will be exercises in this section of the I want you to be intentional about participating in. Taking action is where the true transformation begins.

As we embark and explore the money files, please be intentional and see which of these 12 money files you need to work on the most. Maybe there are some you feel you are doing well with. Maybe your old thought patterns are surfacing and challenging you at this very moment. The little voice in your head is saying "Who do you think you are? You are not good enough!"

The old record player keeps trying to play the same old song that seems to want to sabotage you. It's time to rid yourself of the old paradigm which has kept you broke and living paycheck to paycheck. We are going to work on changing your financial inner economy by being very intentional in this section of the book.

Your financial inner economy overrides your skill set and your knowledge because it is useless if you do not take action.

When was the last time you upgraded your money files?

Americans tend to upgrade their phones every year. We upgrade our computers every few years. We want faster, better technology and programs. The sad part is, we never work on the best computer system in the world – our minds! If you haven't reprogrammed your mind with new money programming, then how do you expect to get different results in your finances? How do you expect to change your relationship with money? How do you expect to attract success? It's going to take new software in your brain.

"Insanity is thinking the same way over and over again expecting different results." Many of us are stuck in a "hope" situation. "I hope my situation gets better." but we never really do the work to be intentional in downloading the new programs we need, the new money files. We never upgrade our financial inner economy from one of a poor-minded person to one of a millionaire-minded person.

As I said earlier in the book, your financial inner economy overrides your skill set and your knowledge because it is useless if you do not take action. Many of us procrastinate because we have a poor-minded financial inner economy.

In the money files, I am going to give you practical steps you can take in your own life. Steps you can implement right away. We are going to examine how millionaires think, the thought processes they go through before they make decisions. Get ready for an amazing journey as we go deeper and become more intentional. It's time to elevate your thinking and living the life you were born to live. Your creator created you to prosper. He gave you dominion over the entire earth. According to your faith be it unto you. I challenge you to activate your faith!

Too many times we focus on the output. How did we get into a situation where we do not have any money in our bank account? How did we get behind on our mortgage, on our rent? We put so much focus on the output that we never focus on the input.

Ladies and gentlemen, it is the input in your mind which determines your output in every area of your life, especially in your finances. Bad information coming in equals bad results coming out. God did not create you to be broke. We serve the God of increase, the God of abundance.

Look at your hands right now. Notice your fingernails. Have you ever wondered why your fingernails continue to grow on their own? We do not have to water them. They just grow by themselves! They grow because that is the very nature, the very character of God.

Look at your hair. Have you ever wondered what makes your hair grow? We don't have to apply any special shampoos to make it grow. We cut our hair often because it grows automatically. It grows by itself. This is the very nature of God. God is the God of multiplication. The human body is a miracle of itself. It's pretty amazing!

Something else which is amazing is the reality that there is no shortage of money in the world. As a matter of fact, there is enough money for everyone to be a millionaire. It is time you get yours. It is time you start paying attention to the habits you have with money.

> *There is enough money for everyone to be a millionaire. It is time you get yours.*

How do you spend your money? What are your money habits? Are you responsible with your money or are you one to go shopping as soon as you see the word "sale"? You might think it's a great deal but it's not. You end up buying multiple items instead of just one. You believe you saved $20, so you go ahead and go buy a second product. The marketing of retailers has conditioned you to buy, to consume more than you need. Retailers are professionals at getting you to pull the trigger and purchase.

Not anymore! The days of buying things you do not need have come to an end. The days of you having new clothes in your closet, which have never been worn, with price tags still on them are over. When you are faithful with a little, you will be entrusted with more. How much money would you have in your savings account if you didn't spend recklessly? $500? $1000? $5000?

Romans 12:2 says, "Be transformed by the renewing of your mind." It takes being intentional and practicing self-discipline. Read these money files over and over, not just once. Repetition is what creates and anchors a new belief system, a new relationship with money.

When your old beliefs try to sneak up on you, you will be able to override them with new ones. The money files are life changing!

I am excited for you to get started! I believe your soul is going to prosper because of the money files. As your soul prospers, you are going to prosper. I can't wait for you to meet the new you!

 Write this down. The future me is counting on me to make the necessary changes I need to make to become the millionaire I was born to be. I was born to make millions!

MONEY FILE #1
MILLIONAIRES TALK ABOUT NET WORTH

Millionaires talk about net worth.
Poor-minded people talk about dollars for hours.

Once I started putting myself in different environments with more successful business owners, I noticed something interesting. I noticed when we were on these high-end golf courses in these high-end country clubs, millionaires were not talking about dollars for hours. They weren't celebrating a $2 an hour raise. The conversations that were happening were about net worth. The conversations at the lunch table revolved around net worth and leaving a legacy for their families.

I remember graduating from high school. At the time, the minimum wage was $3.35 per hour. I was so happy to get paid $5 an hour. I thought I was making a lot of money. We have been taught to believe this lie here in America. We believed that $10 an hour was a lot of money at one time and now, we believe that $20 or $30 an hour is a lot of money. We have been brainwashed to believe this way. Yes, brainwashed!

In reality, it is not. If you think about it, $20 an hour is $41,600 per year. After taxes and Social Security, you don't get to bring home much. Maybe you make $30 an hour and you think that is a lot of money. I challenge your thinking. $30 an hour is $62,400 per year. Remember what we discussed earlier; you need to raise your financial thermostat.

When you start shifting your mindset from thinking about dollars for hours, trading an hour of your time for $20 or $30 an hour, that is where the breakthrough happens for you. You have to stop believing dollars for hours is the way to go. You are never going to build mammoth wealth with the wrong mindset. This is part of the journey of going from a poor-minded financial inner economy to a millionaire-minded financial inner economy.

I want you to start shifting your thinking, shifting your mindset to that of a millionaire mindset. Think about what you want your net worth to be in five years. What do you want your net worth to be in ten years? It is a different language and when you start speaking it, the people and opportunities you attract to yourself will begin to change.

> *I want you to decide right now that where you are currently is not where you are going to be in three years, in five years, in ten years.*

I want you to decide right now that where you are currently is not where you are going to be in three years, in five years, in ten years. When I started on this journey, I had to kill the employee mindset. It was then that we began to see results! Everything began to change.

Maybe you are doubtful because you are currently barely making ends meet. My wife and I argued about money all the time so I understand. I get it. But you have to start somewhere. You have to be intentional. There's that word again! You have to be intentional on creating the changes you want in your finances. You have to be intentional about building your net worth.

Are you in debt right now? Let's say you have $50,000 in credit card debt. How about making the commitment that within three years, you will have a net worth of $100,000?

 Write your future net worth number down. This is why I tell you to keep your journal nearby while reading this book.

Something magical happens when you write things down and put pen to paper. Your subconscious mind has a place to focus, and you accelerate your results.

Get out your journal right now and write down what you want your net worth to be in 3 years. Now write down what you expect your net worth will be in five years. In ten years? And in twenty years?

The law of expectations says, 85% of what we expect, we receive. Implement this law. Expect a certain amount for your net worth. Stop settling for dollars for hours. You are better than that. You are no longer going to be a poor-minded individual. You have the makings of a millionaire mind. Embody the new you.

When you start talking about net worth and legacy and thinking about what you are going to leave behind for your children and grandchildren, it changes the whole trajectory of your life and your business. It gives you something bigger to focus on, to strive towards.

Maybe you have never heard the term net worth. Your net worth is how much you are worth after all your bills and debts have been paid off. How much money do you have in the bank? This goes back to the vision exercise we did earlier with your bank account. How rich do you want to be? Don't be shy now.

If you think back to the exercise we did with the bank statement, how much did you visualize in your bank accounts? This includes investments, stock market accounts, savings accounts, etc.

Remember, you were born to make millions. You were born to make more. I want this thought to be anchored into who you are. Let it soak deep into your core. It's time you create a new paradigm about money and having wealth.

Close your eyes and let's do our vision exercise. Envision the amount of what you want your net worth to be in three years. In five years.

MILLIONAIRE AFFIRMATIONS

"I have a net worth of a quarter-million dollars.
I will have a net worth of half a million dollars in five years.
I will have a net worth of one million dollars in ten years."

Visualize your bank accounts having these amounts of money in them. Doesn't it feel great? Allow yourself to celebrate and feel happy about it. Now you are being intentional.
You may feel uncomfortable with this exercise. Your old mindset may be challenging this thought process right now, you don't even have $5,000 in your bank account and this is

too far-fetched to be realistic. That's okay. Remember, what we focus on expands. When you start focusing on your new net worth, the results are going to show. I will say it again, it's a process.

Take the amount of money you visualized being your net worth in three years and write it on a whiteboard. Put it on a postcard and carry it with you. Put it on an index card and stick it in your car where you will see it. Be intentional.

From this day forward, you are no longer going to focus on trading dollars for hours. This way of thinking is no longer for you. Remember, you are on a journey of becoming and you are becoming a millionaire. These are the makings of a millionaire mind. You are worth the investment. It's time to shift the conversation and start talking about your future net worth. I will see you in the next money file.

Money File #2
MILLIONAIRES TAKE RESPONSIBILITY

Millionaires take responsibility in their lives.
Poor-minded people blame others.

If you want to be a millionaire, you really have to start taking responsibility for your life. You have to take responsibility for everything that is going on in you, around you, in your personal life, in your business and in your relationships. We are quick to blame others. For the past couple of years, we might have blamed COVID. Maybe we have blamed friends, our boss, our spouse, or the economy. We seem to blame everybody and everything except ourselves.

Millionaires look in the mirror and take responsibility for what is going on in their lives, and in their business. We all have a friend or family member who seems to blame everybody else for the bad things going on in their lives. When you see it, you recognize that they are the ones that need to change. When you play the blaming game, you are putting out a negative frequency and all you are doing is attracting more negative situations into your world.

That is not for you anymore. From this day forward, you are a millionaire. You have a millionaire mind. Millionaires take responsibility for their results. I want you to focus on an area in your life that you are not getting the results that you want.

Maybe you started a new workout routine, and the results are just not showing up. Your clothes are not fitting any better and your weight is not where you want it to be. The output in effort does not seem to be generating results.

You might be tempted to blame the workout, or your trainer. You might be complaining that it's too cold or too hot outside so you can't work out. I am going to challenge you to look inside yourself and instead of blaming everything around you, take responsibility for yourself.

"The way we do something is the way we do everything." - Martha Beck

When the results that you want are not showing up, it is time to assess what the problem is. Millionaires look at the results and ask themselves how they can get the results they desire.

> *Millionaires look at the results and ask themselves how they can get the results they desire.*

Remember, the quality of your life is determined by the quality of the questions you ask yourself. Start asking yourself better questions. All that you need is within you now.

Millionaires assess the results and ask themselves these types of questions.

What could I have done differently?

What could I have done better?
Where could I have improved?

Millionaires are honest with themselves. If there is an area where they can improve, they work on that area. Things begin to change the moment you take responsibility for your life and business. Things will begin to shift because no longer are allowing outside circumstances to be an excuse. When you blame others, you are making excuses and blaming the below average results on everybody else.

The easy way out is to cast blame and not take personal responsibility. That is not for you anymore. From this day forward you are going to make the investments you need to make. You are going to take responsibility because you now have a millionaire mind. You are a millionaire.

Close your eyes and envision yourself taking responsibility for your actions. Envision yourself owning the results.

MILLIONAIRE AFFIRMATIONS

"I am a millionaire.
I take responsibility for my results.
I am in control of my life."

Envision the future that you want.

Money File #3
Millionaires Practice Consistency

Millionaires practice consistency.
Poor-minded people always start and stop in life.

One of the main keys to a millionaire's success is they are consistent.

 Write this word down in your notebook now:
CONSISTENCY

Ask yourself this question. How consistent am I? Often, we have a new idea, or a new project and we start working on it because we believe it has a lot of potential. We are excited about it. But after a short period of time, we lose the excitement. Then we stop. I call these start-stops. How many start-stops have you had in your life? How many start-stops have you had on your entrepreneurial journey?

I had to make some big changes in this area to become consistent on a daily basis. Consistency is what wins championships. Consistency is showing up every day regardless if you feel like it or not.

I remember when we started our business, we began posting to the social media platform LinkedIn. I already had quite a few followers on Facebook and a lot of engagement, so I expected the same on LinkedIn. I posted every day for months with no engagement. It was like life was sucked out of me. I wanted to give up. I really did. Nobody was engaging with our content. No one was responding to anything I was posting. It was very disheartening. I was discouraged and I came close to giving up. I felt like a failure. I could not figure out how I had all this interaction on Facebook yet nothing on LinkedIn.

I want you to shift your mind and start thinking long-term. Millionaires are consistent because they think long-term.

I gave myself 6 months. I committed to posting on LinkedIn every day for six months, regardless of the engagement. I was not going to worry about the outcome. Lo and behold, God rewarded my consistency. Suddenly I saw hope at the end of the tunnel. All the posts I had created compounded, and one day a post just exploded. I was shocked. It really encouraged me and built up my confidence. It took approximately six months to get to this point. I was crying tears of joy. I had really wanted to give in.

Reflect on your life. How many start-stops have you had this month? This year?

I want you to shift your mind and start thinking long-term. Millionaires are consistent because they think long-term. They know their efforts are going to be rewarded and they know that if they show up every single day on a consistent basis, consistency wins. Consistency is one of the key factors to a millionaire's success.

What if I had only posted on LinkedIn for three months and then stopped? All the momentum I had built up would have been wasted. What if I had stopped and taken some time to get professional advice from a social media expert? They would have advised me to give it six to twelve months and to start it up again. I would have had to start back at the beginning with no momentum and it

> *It takes more energy to start all over again when all the momentum is lost.*

would have been twice as hard to get it going again. I would have lost all the energy and efforts I had invested.

It takes more energy to start all over again when all the momentum is lost. I want to encourage you, as you are reading this money file today, to pay attention to these start-stops. Every time you start something and then stop again, you lose so much momentum. The only person you are hurting is yourself. If you are a business owner, you are hurting your employees. You have to be consistent, to show up every single day even if you do not feel like it.

Believe me, I know it is not easy. I have been in a place where I have wanted to give up. I felt like a failure. Winston Churchill once said, "Success is going from failure to failure without the loss of enthusiasm." Don't lose your enthusiasm! Don't lose the excitement!

As you are developing and building your life of abundance and wealth, understand you have to be consistent in everything you do. You have to be consistent and pay yourself first. It may not look like a lot of money in your savings account or a lot of money in your freedom account, but you have to understand the more consistent you are, the better results you will see.

Stop being so hard on yourself. That's why we stop. We are hard on ourselves when we don't see the results we want. Stop beating yourself up.

Sometimes, I still have to keep myself from beating myself up. Decide today that you will no longer beat yourself up. Decide today you are showing up no matter what! Half of success is just showing up and being there. As you are planting the seeds, over time, the results you desire will come. The winning results will show up.

Millionaires are consistent regardless of the circumstances around them. Learn to be consistent and not allow circumstances to derail you. I see many young entrepreneurs get off track because of one loss, one setback. They make a long-life decision based on one event. Use wisdom. You are better than that. Millionaires never give up. You, my friend, are a millionaire.

Close your eyes and envision yourself being consistent. Envision yourself showing up every single day at the gym, eating healthier, etc. Envision yourself being consistent in building up your freedom account. How does it feel to be winning BIG in life and business?

MILLIONAIRE AFFIRMATIONS

"I am consistency.
I am consistent.
I am showing up every day to attract millions into my
bank account. "

Envision those $100 bills flowing into your bank accounts. It feels amazing, doesn't it? Consistency wins ladies and gentlemen!

You deserve to win. You deserve to be wealthy. You deserve to be rich to help others. Give yourself the gift of consistency. I will see you at the next money file.

Money File # 4
Millionaires
Celebrate Others

Millionaires celebrate others.
Poor-minded people are jealous of others.

This money file hits home. To be totally transparent with you, this is something I struggled with as God was growing me and developing me to become a millionaire. Regardless of how much success we had in business, I would find myself being jealous of others. I did not understand why. If I, Daniel, was doing great growing our business, why did I see myself reacting to a social media post in a negative manner? The reason was because of my insecurities.

One valuable lesson I learned from being around millionaires and very successful people is they celebrate other people's victories. They celebrate other people's wins. What does this look like? Not celebrating others.

When you see a post on social media, does your stomach get tied up in knots? Do you find yourself feeling jealous of that person? Do you accuse them of showing off or bragging? Maybe you feel this way because of the insecurities you have within yourself.

It is time for a self-assessment. If you are finding yourself being jealous and envious of a person's social media post, you are probably doing the same thing in other areas of your life.

Learn how to celebrate the victories of other people.

I had to become intentional in celebrating others. The more I did it, the easier it became, and I learned how to genuinely feel happy for other people. I enjoy hosting aspiring speakers at our "Sticker Shock Speaking Academy." I would love for them to attend 2 or 3 more times. But, they grow as individuals, they grow as speakers. And because they grow, some start having their own events.

I had to learn how to celebrate their victories and cheer them on at a deeper level. Seeing our speakers host their own events is priceless. It fills my heart with happiness! Where in your life are you being poor-minded and jealous of other people?

You need to learn how to celebrate the victories of other people. How often do you struggle to celebrate other people? Today, as you go through your day, think about a way you can be intentional in celebrating others. Start with a small celebration and work your way up to a big one. Maybe you begin with wishing someone a happy birthday. Reach out to them and leave them a voice message. If you know someone who just got a big win in their business, call them up and celebrate with them. Send them a celebratory text message. This is how you develop your millionaire mind.

When you are happy for others and you learn how to celebrate them, it attracts abundance to you. It tells success you are maturing, and success comes your way. God sees your heart and he will bless you with more. Don't allow jealousy and envy to keep you from what God has in store for you. Jealousy will kill your dreams and keep you stuck at your current level. It is like walking into a huge office building with a revolving door and you can't go in or out, you just keep going in circles. As much as you want to get out of the doorway, you can't. You are stuck in a revolving door. The key to getting unstuck is to be genuinely happy for other people. Everyone needs encouragement. Everyone deserves recognition. Everyone deserves to be celebrated!

The truth is not everyone is going to celebrate your success and your wins. You need to be ok with it. You are not the same person anymore and some people will not like it. This was a hard pill for me to swallow and accept.

When friends and family who are close to you post passive-aggressive comments on social media, maybe they are directing their negative energy towards you or maybe they're not. This is where you need to understand as you start to develop your millionaire mind, your new way of thinking is elevating your frequency to higher levels. Most people choose to live on the lower frequencies. They choose to be average and average people tend to get jealous.

You have to learn not to take things personally. This was a hard lesson for me to learn.

Close your eyes. Envision yourself celebrating other people's victories. Think of a friend or family member you want to celebrate today. Visualize yourself celebrating a friend's promotion at work. Visualize yourself congratulating your family member on their new car! Doesn't it feel great to celebrate people's wins?

MILLIONAIRE AFFIRMATIONS

"Millionaires celebrate others.
I am a millionaire.
I am celebrating others."

Go out there today and be intentional in celebrating others. Be intentional in recognizing and appreciating the people around you who support you.

If you are a business owner, celebrate your employees. If you want your business to grow, celebrate, appreciate, and recognize your employees.

MONEY FILE #5
MILLIONAIRES DEAL WITH THE HARD ISSUES

Millionaires deal with the hard issues.
Poor-minded people sweep them under the rug.

I think it is human nature to avoid dealing with hard issues. We don't want to deal with the elephants in the room. But the reality is, in order to grow and obtain mammoth wealth, we have to deal with these hard issues in life and in business. Millionaires tackle the elephants in the room head-on.

Poor-minded people are overwhelmed when they see the elephant in the room. They will take the path of least resistance and not even deal with it. Many of us don't even acknowledge it. We sweep it under the rug and hope it goes away.

Ask yourself, "What hard issues in life am I not working through right now?" You might be using the excuse "I don't like conflict." I am no different from you. Honestly, most people do not like conflict. When I was younger, I did not want to deal with these hard issues. I did not want to talk about it. My solution was to get angry. That was my only defense mechanism to avoid having to talk about it. I can remember breaking a wine glass or two, not that I am proud of it, I am just being honest about the issues I had to deal with as I was growing and becoming a millionaire. You have to go deeper inside yourself and heal all your unresolved issues. They will be different for every individual.

At some point in your life, all these problems you swept under the rug and stuffed in the closet must be dealt with.

I want you to know that you are dreaming if you think these problems are never going to have to be addressed. At some point in your life, all these problems you swept under the rug and stuffed in the closet must be dealt with. They will keep resurfacing and cause you to feel undeserving and guilty.

I am not a counselor, but I can tell you I do understand money and finances. You will carry the same unresolved money triggers from relationship to relationship until you deal with the hard issues. Relationships with your children, spouse, colleagues, and employees are all affected. One thing I had to learn how to do as a millionaire was deal with my unresolved conflicts and problems from the past. It was so freeing once I did.

Shame will never disappear until you defeat it.

As I was growing and progressing to get to the next level in my business, I did need another business coach. I asked God for his help to find the specific type of coach I needed for this season. He led me to my amazing coach, Karen. I have hired many coaches, but Karen helped me conquer what was blocking me from my next level of success. She helped me discover what was hindering me by teaching me how to overcome the shame.

I can tell you, as a millionaire myself, shame will never disappear until you defeat it. It's the shame we carry with us that we never talk about. We continue to sweep it under the rug, and it never gets resolved. It's hurting you more by ignoring it than if you just exposed it.

In one of my coaching sessions with Karen, the light came on for me. I realized I had never forgiven myself for attempting suicide. I had never forgiven myself for shooting myself in my abdominal area trying to end my life. More than 30 years after my suicide attempt, I was still holding on to the shame. I was unaware of it. In that session, I forgave myself. It was so powerful because I released the shame that had been killing the creativity in my life. I exposed the shame by sharing my story on stage at our Sticker Shock Speaking Academy. It opened other people to talk about the shame they were feeling in their lives. It was so empowering!

 Grab your notebook and write this question down: What shame from my past have I not dealt with?

I had to forgive myself for something I had done more than 30 years ago. Maybe you had a loved one that died, and you feel ashamed because you were not there for them. You never got a chance to say your last goodbye. Maybe it's the shame of not being the mother or father you needed to be to your children. Whatever it is for you, deal with it!

As a young leader of a multi-million-dollar organization, I made a lot of mistakes. I had many employees who were depending on me. I let them down and allowed the shame to build up for many years. I had to forgive myself for all my failures and release the shame and regrets.

Right now, I need you to lead yourself. Remember, millionaires deal with hard issues. What hard issue are you not dealing with?

Maybe you made a bad investment with your money. I remember when the dot com was booming many years ago. I made an investment in Juno. It was like Yahoo back in the day. I invested thousands of dollars and when the dot com bubble burst, I lost thousands of dollars. I had to learn to forgive myself for that. It's not worth holding on to past failures ladies and gentlemen. The shame is what makes you believe you are unworthy and undeserving of becoming a millionaire.

What financial decision have you made that is causing you to carry shame with you? One of my friends had a beautiful home. We lived in the same neighborhood for many years. A nicer, more prominent subdivision was being built near where we lived. Their current beautiful house was almost paid off. He took the equity from that house and bought the new one.

I believe when you make a decision based on vanity, with the wrong motives, sometimes things do not work out the way you hoped they would. 2008 came along and the economy crashed. The crash affected millions of people in our country. They foreclosed on their new home. He ended up losing it. I felt bad for him because I could see the shame eating him up inside.

Maybe you have had a similar experience? We have all experienced shame on one level or another. Release your shame today and forgive yourself. I have failed many times. I have had to forgive myself each time. If you have made some bad decisions with money, it's time you forgive yourself. The shame is keeping you from being the millionaire you were born to be. I want you to stop sweeping things under the rug. I want you to start dealing with the unresolved issues. I want you to start attacking those elephants in the room instead of walking around them. It is time you deal with the shame that is holding you back from your success.

I can honestly tell you it has brought me so much freedom. When I dealt with the hard issues, our business started skyrocketing. Our revenue grew. Everything accelerated. God accelerated our business. God blessed everything we were doing. I share my story with you because this is something I personally went through, and I have seen it hinder so many of my clients who do not deal with their shame.

Close your eyes. Envision yourself dealing with the hard issues. Envision yourself releasing the shame and the guilt in your life.

MILLIONAIRE AFFIRMATIONS

"Millionaires deal with the hard issues in life.
Millionaires release their shame.
I am a millionaire."

Today you have decided to play all-in, and I thank you. I believe this is one of the most powerful money files. I will see you at the next one.

Money File #6
MILLIONAIRES SPEAK LIFE

Millionaires speak life.
Poor-minded people speak death.

We all have the one friend or co-worker we know as "Negative Nancy." You know the one? The person who is always negative about everything. They ooze negativity. Poor-minded individuals speak death over themselves, and they don't even realize it. They are cursing themselves and their future. On the flipside of the coin, millionaires speak life. They speak life over their own lives, they speak life over their business and their relationships. They especially speak life over their finances.

Let me put this into perspective for you. When a millionaire wakes up, they say "It is going to be a great day today. Something amazing is going to happen today. I am having a great day in business today. All good things come to me. Everything is going right for me!"

That is what speaking life looks like. On the other hand, you have the poor-minded individual who says "Nothing ever goes right for me. Business is slow. What else can go wrong? This is too good to be true." The poor-minded focus on the negative.

They never develop the millionaire's attitude where they speak positivity over themselves.

I want you to see yourself as an artist right now. I want to paint this picture for you. You are an artist. Every day, as an artist, you are given a white canvas. That white canvas is your day. Every day you are given a magical paintbrush to paint on the canvas. The magical paintbrush represents the words you speak daily. The picture you paint for the day is created by the magical paintbrush of your words. That is the picture you are painting for your life. Six months ago, a year ago, five years ago, you painted the picture of the life you are living right now. You painted it with the words you spoke. This is how powerful your words are.

Life and death are in the power of the tongue.

The Great Book of Wisdom says, "Life and death are in the power of the tongue." What are you speaking on a daily basis? Are you speaking life or are you speaking death into existence?

The picture millionaires paint for themselves is a picture of life. They have been intentional. There's that word INTENTIONAL again! They have been intentional in painting a picture of success, abundance, love, and increase. Millionaires paint a picture of wealth!

Poor-minded individuals have been painting a picture of lack and scarcity. They paint a picture of excuses and alibis. They don't even realize it. Their poor-minded financial inner economy is running their life and habitually making decisions for them.

Our decisions, the words we speak daily, are governed by our financial inner economy. Start paying attention to the pictures you are painting for your life. Become more aware of what you are saying!

Millionaires speak life over themselves.

Make a conscious decision from this day forward that you are going to start speaking life over yourself because you are a millionaire. You have the makings of a millionaire mind inside of you. All that you need is within you now.

MILLIONAIRE AFFIRMATIONS

"I am valuable.
I am chosen.
I am approved.
I am loved and accepted by God.
I am amazing.
I am forgiven."

Close your eyes as we do the vision exercise. Envision yourself speaking life over every area of your life and business.

Feel the positive energy coming from the words you are speaking. Speak life over your sales department. Speak life over your revenue. Speak life over your health.

Now I want you to put your name in place of the word "I" in the above millionaire affirmations. What I say is "Daniel is valuable. Daniel is chosen. Daniel is approved. Daniel is loved and accepted by God. Daniel is amazing. Daniel is forgiven.

Daniel is worthy. Daniel is deserving." Envision yourself being worthy and deserving. Doesn't it feel amazing?

As you open your eyes after doing this exercise, I want you to start speaking life over yourself throughout the day. Start blessing your life instead of cursing it. When you speak negative about yourself, you are cursing yourself. Put an end to the insanity.

It is time you start seeing yourself as valuable. Most people never become millionaires because they do not value who they are. They undervalue themselves. And when you undervalue how you see yourself, then the marketplace will never see any value in you. In order to become a millionaire, you have to see yourself as being of great value.

Money File #7
Millionaires Work for Themselves

Millionaires work for themselves.
Poor-minded people work for others.

One of the big differences between millionaires, the middle class and poor-minded people is that millionaires bet on themselves. They start their own businesses. They go out on a limb. They do not allow the opinions of other people to keep them from pursuing their dreams and really doing what God has put on their hearts. Poor-minded and middle-class people build their lives on a foundation of security. I believe you can have too much security in your life. The poor-minded and middle class want everything to be perfect and secure.

We found this out in 2020 when COVID took us out of our comfort zones. You might have been at your job for 10 years, 20 years, or even longer and suddenly hundreds of thousands lost their jobs due to covid. Americans learned no job was secure regardless of their tenure. Poor-minded and middle-class people have a false sense of security in their jobs. There is no such thing as job security!

Millionaires work for themselves because they understand what it takes to become a millionaire. There is no limitation on the amount of money you can earn when you work for yourself. There are no limits!

You have a gift inside of you, something you love to do.

When you work for somebody else, when you work from 9 to 5, you are limited by your hourly wage or salary. Let's say you work for $10 per hour, $20, or even $30 per hour. $30 an hour sounds like a lot of money, but the truth is it is only $60,000 per year. Even making $30 an hour, you are never going to become wealthy. You are never going to become super-rich because there is a limit on how many hours you can work in a day. There is a limit on how many hours you can work in a week. Trading your hours for dollars limits your income capabilities.

You need to remove the lid limiting the amount of money you can earn. Even if you get paid a salary, your income has a cap. It has limitations.

To be successful, to be rich and become a millionaire, to develop the makings of the millionaire mind, I want you to understand you need to bet on yourself and not be scared to go after the dream inside your heart. You have a gift inside of you, something you love to do.

I followed the dream inside of me. That's what got me to where I am today, a successful millionaire. Even though people laughed at me, even though they thought I was crazy, I bet on myself. People questioned me "Do you know how many Hispanic motivational speakers there are Daniel?" Against all odds, I was crazy enough to believe in myself. I was crazy enough to bet on myself and follow my heart in becoming a professional speaker. I took action and never looked back!

I didn't earn as much money the first couple of years after starting my business, as a motivational speaker, as when I worked in the automotive industry. But I refused to let it discourage me or deter me from accomplishing what God put on my heart to do.

As you transition from a 9-5 job and working for other people, to becoming an entrepreneur, you need to think long-term. Stop thinking short-term. Poor-minded and middle-class people only focus on the immediate results, the immediate gratification. I never focused on the $200,000 per year position I left behind. I focused on the earning potential of our business, and it paid off!

I followed what I loved to do. Within a few years, we had surpassed what I was making in the automotive industry.

Take a moment to consider what it is you love to do. If you are working for someone else, I am going to bet there is a good probability you dislike your job. There are thousands of people working 9-5 who hate their current job. JOB stands for Just Over Broke. I encourage you to dream bigger for yourself.

 We serve a limitless God. You are limitless! Write down this word right now in your journal.
LIMITLESS

I want you to declare this right now. Say it out loud. "I am limitless." That is you! And when you come to the realization you are limitless because you serve a limitless God, there is nothing you cannot accomplish with the right discipline and the right focus. Since you are limitless and our God is limitless, then your income is limitless.

I often get approached by people who want me to join their multi-level marketing team. I refuse their invitations because I am convinced that I have found my lane. In business, understand you need to run your own race. You must stay in your own lane. Staying in my lane has helped me to excel. I am intentional in conducting business in my expertise. Regardless of the opportunities that came my way, I do not allow distractions to get me off course.

Remember, not all that glitters is gold.

Remember, not all that glitters is gold.

Take this money file to heart because it's going to help you see where you are in life. You might be over 40 years old. Do not let age be an excuse. I was in the automotive industry for almost 20 years. I was 44 years old when I made the decision to become a motivational speaker.

In addition to my keynote speaking, we now train aspiring speakers who want to get paid to speak at our Sticker Shock Speaking Academy. One success led to another.

The Daniel Gomez Inspires Show was born, and we won Podcast of the Year in 2020. Because we won podcast of the year, we started helping podcasters launch their podcasts and build their brands. Then our business coaching exploded with our Shield of Faith Coaching. People wanted to know what we were doing and how we were doing it. They started reaching out for help.

All of our success came from being intentional and not allowing people to distract me. I didn't care about other people's opinions. I was too busy focusing on staying in my lane and running my race. Today, if you are unhappy at your job and this money file resonated with you, I want you to be bold enough to ask God to guide you.

Maybe you are saying "Daniel, I don't believe in God." Hey, I get it. That was me when I was younger. I was put in a situation where my dad was diagnosed with cancer, and they only gave him a couple of weeks to live. Crying, I remember bargaining with God "If you are real, help my dad and I will serve you." And boy, did God show me He was real! They gave my dad a month to live, but because of God's grace he lived another year. He can do the same for you.

There is a real God waiting to hear from you.

Close your eyes. Envision yourself doing what you love. What does that look like to you right now? Envision yourself monetizing your God-given gifts.

Maybe you are a florist or a baker, maybe you are an artist or a designer. Envision yourself being your own boss, having your own business. It's amazing. How does it feel?

MILLIONAIRE AFFIRMATIONS

"I am limitless.
I declare my income is limitless.
I am a millionaire. "

You are limitless. Your income is limitless. You are becoming a millionaire.

Money File #8
Millionaires Buy What They Want

Millionaires buy what they want.
Poor-minded people look at prices.

How many times have you gone into the department store and fallen in love with an item you wanted? It was love at first sight. But you looked at the price tag and it was more than what you wanted to spend. You ended up leaving the item there at the store. Then you leave and while driving home, you are thinking to yourself "I should have just bought it."

That was me, the old Daniel Gomez. I remember so many times I saw something I wanted and even at times something I needed, and I would not buy it because it was more than I was willing to pay. I will never forget when we moved into our new home, I wanted lion statues. The previous owners had lion statues in the front of the yard. They looked nice! I searched for these lion statues for about two months, and I could not find them. I finally found the perfect ones. They were exactly what I had been wanting.

When we went to pick them up, there were some smaller lions beside the ones I ordered. I suggested to my wife that maybe the smaller ones would suffice. After some consideration, I backed out of buying any lion statues at all, regardless of size. I decided I didn't need them.

Your financial inner economy trumps all knowledge and skills. It can keep you from taking action.

Then my wife said something that hit me right in my heart. She said, "Daniel, buy the lions you want. You deserve them." I was about to settle for something much less or even do without because of the price point. I want you to understand millionaires buy what they want.

I had to grow into my millionaire mind. There will be situations which come your way that you will need to push through. Your poor-minded financial inner economy will try and hold you back. My experience in purchasing these lions is an example of the type of situation that helped me to create a millionaire-minded financial inner economy. Remember what I have been saying all along? Your financial inner economy trumps all knowledge and skills. It can keep you from taking action.

You have to be intentional about making decisions. Ladies and gentlemen, millionaires do not look at the prices. They buy what they want. This was a process I had to work through myself. I'm so happy now when I drive up to our home and I see our lions in front of our beautiful home. They bring a smile to my face. I want to encourage you today to stop looking at prices. If you want something, buy it.

How many times have you gone out to lunch with friends and instead of buying what you want, you order the lunch special? In many cases, what you really want to eat is just slightly higher priced than the special. I have been guilty of this myself. Now, when I go out to eat, I order what I want.

When you go out to eat, stop settling for a meal you don't want. The more you make it a habit, the easier it gets. The next time you go out for a meal, I want you to stretch yourself and order the item that may be a few dollars more. I'm going to take it a step further and ask you to go outside your comfort zone. I challenge you to have dinner at a higher-end restaurant. I want you to order something to eat that you don't normally order. This experience should stretch you and make you feel a little uncomfortable. The objective of this assignment is to build your millionaire-minded financial inner economy.

I was recently speaking with one of my coaching clients. He wanted to stretch himself. He was tired of living life in survival mode. He told me he would put $10 worth of gas in his car every other day. I asked him why he didn't just fill up his gas tank? He felt it cost too much to fill it up. His homework assignment was to fill his car's gas tank up. The more he did it, the easier it got. Before he knew it, filling up his gas tank became the new normal.

The more you start to believe you are worth it, knowing you are God's child, and He wants good things for you, you are going to go out there and not be scared to reward yourself!

This is a great example of how poor-minded people think without even being aware of it. Millionaires don't think this way. Millionaires fill up their tanks with gas. Millionaires don't look at prices. There is a millionaire inside of you that is trying to come out. Remember, you are in the process of building your millionaire-minded financial inner economy.

I want to challenge you today. The next time you go on vacation, stay at a nicer hotel. Maybe you have gone on vacation, and you've wanted to stay at the Hilton or stay at a luxury resort, but you've always chosen to go with a cheaper option. Another client of mine and I were talking about this, and I told him "You have to kill your Motel 6 mentality." The Motel 6 mentality is a scarcity poverty mindset. I told him the next time he went on vacation, I wanted him to stretch himself and stay at a nicer hotel.

The more you practice buying what you want, the easier it gets. When you make decisions for the right reasons and with the right motives, everything around you elevates. Kill that Motel 6 mentality. Go out there and stay at a Hilton, stay at a Marriott or a resort that you would not normally stay at. Allow yourself to experience the new in your life.

When we stayed at the Ritz-Carlton for the first time, it was amazing and so beautiful. It was not easy to spend that much money and it definitely took me out of my comfort zone. Once I put myself in that environment and purchased what I wanted, it was a great feeling. It gets easier and easier every time I do it. Millionaires understand this truth. Millionaires understand that there are going to be challenges as they grow and stretch their belief systems.

Millionaires believe they are worth it. And you are worth it! The more you start to believe you are worth it, knowing you are God's child, and He wants good things for you, you are going to go out there and not be scared to reward yourself. You are not going to be scared to treat yourself. As you get ready to book your next trip or your next getaway, no more

Motel 6's, no more Super 8's. Stretch yourself. A stretched mind and a stretched belief system cannot retract back to its original size.

Close your eyes. I want you to envision yourself walking into the mall or department store and buying what you want. Visualize yourself trying on the outfit you've been wanting. Can you see yourself wearing it home? Visualize yourself buying those things you have always wanted. Doesn't it feel amazing to buy what you want?

Open your eyes.

MILLIONAIRE AFFIRMATIONS

"I can afford anything that I want.
I can afford anything that my heart desires.
I am a millionaire.
I am super rich.
I was born to make millions. "

I don't want you to get this money file out of context. I'm not saying to be foolish and selfish with your money. I'm saying many poor-minded people never reward themselves. They never celebrate their achievements. You deserve to be celebrated. You are a millionaire. Millionaires celebrate themselves.

Money File #9
Millionaires Act in Spite of Not Having All the Answers

Millionaires act in spite of not having all the answers.
Poor-minded people want all the answers up front.

How many times has an opportunity come your way, something that you have been praying for or wanting, and the opportunity is presented right there in the palm of your hand, and you don't take it? The opportunity slips right through your fingers.

Because of you being poor-minded and wanting all the answers up front, you missed it. Millionaires act in spite of having all the answers. Millionaires do not need to have all the details before they act. It's time you stopped missing these opportunities that God brings into your life, that you have been praying for, because of that poor-minded financial inner economy.

Millionaires act in spite of fear. Believe me, I have been scared many times to make some of the decisions that I have made. There has been fear and doubt, but I have learned that everything I want is on the other side of Daniel not having all the answers. The desires of my heart are on the other side of acting in spite of fear. This was an intentional step towards building my millionaire mindset.

> *The desires of my heart are on the other side of acting in spite of fear.*

I remember when God put the dream in my heart of becoming a motivational speaker. I was going upstairs to get dressed for an interview at an automotive dealership to go run it. As I was getting dressed, I found this old email that a school counselor had sent me from one of the moms. It read like this: "Who is this car guy? Who is this gentleman that spoke to my son at the school? My son is running around yelling and screaming." At this point while I was reading the email I thought "Oh crap, what did I do?"

The email continued to say "Tell him I said thank you. My son has never been happier. EJ looks in the mirror and tells himself 'I love myself and I believe in myself.' He puts on this Chevrolet cap and he's never been more confident. Tell him I said thank you."

As I read this email, I knew God was calling me to be a motivational speaker. I was excited! I was thrilled! All of us experience that excitement when we first get a glimpse of work that we love. I went and told my wife and she thought that I was crazy. I continued forward in spite of not having all the answers. Think about this for a moment. I had run multimillion-dollar automotive dealerships for 20 years and I had no idea about the industry of speaking. But I was crazy enough to trust God and activate my faith. Even though I did not have all the answers up front, I took action.

Today, you need to take action on some things. You need to take action on some of those things that you have had on the shelf for a long time that you know you should have started on by now. Part of developing this millionaire mindset is taking action without having all the answers. You are not poor-minded anymore. That version of you is no longer in existence. You have a millionaire mind. You have the makings of a millionaire mind inside of you right now.

I want you to tap into that boldness. Tap into that decisiveness and take action in spite of not having all the answers. You are a millionaire. And the same way I took action on my motivational speaking career, is the same way you are going to act today. No longer will you tolerate being poor-minded.

As I look back now, what would have happened had I not taken action? I would have missed out on writing this book that you are reading right now. It would have never existed because I would not have had the idea of becoming an author.

> *I want you to tap into your boldness.*

I became an author because I went to a speaker training where I met an author there for the first time in person. I was amazed to meet someone who had written a book. I thought that was the best thing!

When I came back from that training, I did not share that with anybody. But the seed had been planted. Meeting this author and seeing the excitement and joy that he had about this book that he had written inspired me. I thought to myself how cool it would be to be an author.

Once again, Daniel Gomez did not have all the answers in becoming an author or how to publish a book. But I started asking questions. I started being nosey. I started inquiring and

I had so many different opportunities come to me in reference to the publishing aspect of my first book, *You Were Born to Fly*. I had three options. I almost refused to take any of those three because I did not have all the answers up front. I did not know how to write a book or how I was going to pay for it. Honestly, I was scared.

In spite of not having all of the answers, I continued moving forward. I knew that on the other side of having all the answers was where my first book was going to be born.

I am no better than you. I just put in the work to kill that poor-minded financial inner economy inside of me and to develop that millionaire-minded financial inner economy. I was intentional about going from a poor man's financial DNA to a millionaire's financial DNA.

Decide today that you are going to act in spite of not having all the answers. You are a millionaire.

Close your eyes. I want you to envision an opportunity that you had and maybe you missed it. Or maybe it's a new opportunity for you. Envision it coming your way. Maybe it is a new job, a new career, maybe it is starting your own business or maybe it is going back to school. Whatever it might be for you, envision it for yourself. See yourself taking action and feeling great about the decision that you have made. It is amazing. Envision yourself taking action. Doesn't that feel amazing?

Open your eyes.

MILLIONAIRE AFFIRMATIONS

"I am acting in spite of not having all the answers.
Millionaires act in spite of not having all the answers.
I am a millionaire.
I am taking action today.
I am super-rich.
I was born to make millions. "

I am proud of you. Thank you for playing all in and reading this amazing book up to this point. Your life is changing.

Congratulations!

Money File #10
Millionaires Are Relentless

Millionaires are relentless.
Poor-minded people get frustrated and distracted.

I have a question for you as we start this money file. Are you easily frustrated? Are you easily distracted?

Poor-minded people get easily frustrated when things do not go their way. They get frustrated when things get challenging. They get frustrated when the pressure is on. Millionaires are relentless. Millionaires are determined. Millionaires turn on that extra gear inside of them and they overcome the frustrations and distractions. You, my friend, are a millionaire. From this day forward, I want you to decide to be relentless. I want you to be committed to being relentless.

I have seen many people that get so easily frustrated. When you get frustrated, it distorts your thinking. It kills your creativity and blocks your thinking. Maybe you are wondering why you have not gotten further in life, and in your business. The dreams that you had as a young entrepreneur are fading because you get easily frustrated. Millionaires understand that they have to stay focused and be relentless. They have to get back up from failures. They have to get back up from setbacks.

Ladies and gentlemen, the failures are going to come. Setbacks are going to happen. The question is, how are you handling these setbacks? How are you handling the failures?

 Write this quote from the great Winston Churchill down in your notebook:
"Success is going from failure to failure without the loss of enthusiasm."

My wife had just finished her first major surgery, a double mastectomy. She was stable and starting to feel better. She had a follow-up appointment with her doctor a week after the surgery. As we walked into the doctor's office, we sensed the aura of a bad feeling. It was in the air. It was in the doctor's tone of voice as he began speaking with us.

I will never forget his words. "The good news is that the surgery went well but there is some cancer remaining on the left side of your chest. It looks as if the cancer cells have spread onto your skin." I grasped my wife's hand. It felt like we had been punched hard in the stomach. We started crying. We had just been in surgery a week prior to that. As we sat there with tears in our eyes and our heads hanging low, I didn't have any answers again.

I remember crying out to God asking him to give us wisdom.

And He did.

He said "Be relentless my son. Keep going forward. Mari is in my hands. I am protecting and guiding her." I told my wife that evening, "Let's forget about everything and go enjoy a night out at the movies. Let's enjoy ourselves." We watched a

Christmas movie there at the theater. It was a beautiful evening.

Despite the news that we had gotten that afternoon, we continued forward, and we were relentless. Mari was relentless. As I look back, I realize now that a big part of the success that I have had in business and in our lives came from Mari. My wife never played the victim. She never asked, "Why me?" Instead, she asked, "Why not me?" She was relentless in her pursuit to not allow breast cancer to take her down.

> *You can't expect to be at the highest level when it is something that is new to you. So instead of telling yourself that you are frustrated, and this is hard, tell yourself I am fascinated, and this is exciting.*

I want you to take a moment and think about an area in your life where you need to practice being relentless. Do you need to stop getting so easily frustrated? Do you need to stop getting so easily distracted? I want you to stop saying the word frustrated. I am going to share with you a millionaire mind hack. I want you to start saying "I am fascinated." That moment when you feel yourself getting frustrated, I want you to proclaim, "I am fascinated!"

I've been there. I am no different than you. With all the growth we have experienced, I found myself at one time saying I was frustrated. It is going to be challenging because we are doing new things that we have never done. You can't expect to be at the highest level when it is something that is new to you. So instead of telling yourself that you are frustrated, and this is hard, tell yourself I am fascinated, and this is exciting.

That is the way a millionaire thanks. That is the makings of a millionaire mind in progress. Embrace this mind hack and start telling yourself "This is fascinating."

You are a millionaire.

Close your eyes. I want you to envision yourself being relentless. I want you to envision yourself making one more sales call for your business, one more push-up, one more set in your workout. Envision yourself being relentless and an amazing spouse to your partner. You are not getting frustrated any longer. Envision yourself feeling fascinated. Embrace the growth. Embrace the challenges. You are going to learn something new in life. Envision yourself winning. Winners are relentless. That is you. Doesn't it feel amazing to be relentless and not give up so easily? Doesn't it feel great to not get frustrated and distracted?

Open your eyes.

MILLIONAIRE AFFIRMATIONS

"I am a relentless millionaire.
I am relentless.
I am fascinated every day.
I am a millionaire.
I am super-rich.
I was born to make millions."

MONEY FILE #11
MILLIONAIRES PRIORITIZE THEIR LIVES

Millionaires prioritize their lives.

This is a bonus money file that I want to give to you. It's actually my personal money file. It helped me to reach the level of success that I have achieved. Often, we listen to what the world says in reference to our careers, our business, and how we handle our finances. The truth is we have it all out of order. It's out of whack.

Maybe you have been going through this book and doing all the exercises, but you are still feeling like your life is out of whack. We all have our own definitions of wealth and success. For me, the true breakthrough to the next level of the millionaire realm was the decision to put God first in my life and in my business. I was putting him first in my life but when it came to the business, I was trying to do everything on my own.

Maybe in your career and business, you have been trying to do everything on your own and you have made yourself the CEO of your organization. Three years ago, we were experiencing some steady growth. One morning while I was in prayer, God asked me "Are you going to run this business or am I going to run this business? Daniel, you are busy doing nothing."

Ouch. I was trying to do it all. I was trying to force a square peg into a circular hole. Maybe things have not been clicking for you in business. Maybe things have not been growing at the rate that you would like them to. The answer was asking God to run my business for me.

> *The moment I humbled myself to receive from God the instructions, the guidance, and the blueprint for our business, our business grew exponentially.*

That week, I went to my LinkedIn profile and God became the CEO of my business. He became the CEO of Daniel Gomez Enterprises. This may sound far-fetched to you, but it is the truth. I demoted myself to the president. In my humor, I said "Well God, can I be the president?" He replied, "You can be whatever you want to be but you're not going to be the CEO if you want this business to flourish, son."

The moment I humbled myself to receive from God the instructions, the guidance, and the blueprint for our business, our business grew exponentially.

We all know what happened in 2020 when many businesses closed and laid off people. We were growing. We doubled in size in 2020. I implemented the ideas and strategies that God gave me.

Maybe for the past year, you have been trying to execute your strategies and ideas in business and they are just not working. Are you being stubborn trying to do it on your own? Your way may not be the right way.

Then again, in 2021, God brought us amazing people to help us to grow and now we are scaling. I started understanding business at a new level. The ideas that were being downloaded during my time with God in the mornings were just amazing. In 2021, we doubled our business again.

When I really prioritized my life and put God first, sought His wisdom, guidance, and strategies, miracles started happening. It is like God's blessings were chasing me down. God's wealth was chasing me down. I was attracting the right people. After I made God CEO, instead of me chasing success and chasing wealth, it seems success and wealth began chasing me down. Opportunities chased me down.

This is a different way of thinking. We often hear lies on social media or on podcasts, sometimes from so-called prominent influencers, that the answer to success is to rise and grind and hustle all day. What type of life is that? You can't enjoy success if you're always grinding and moving at the speed of light. Look at the word itself: grinding. Who wants to be grinding all day? That does not sound attractive.

When you are operating from your God-given gift, when you have tapped into the source of life and the source of your very creation, and you put the most-high God in control, that's when the real breakthroughs come.

Never in my life did I ever dream that I would be in the position that I am. It is all because of God. What I did in my life to become the millionaire that I am today is that I truly put God first and everything that I did. God became the CEO of my life and of my business.

 Get out your notebook and write in your notes:
GOD FIRST

The second thing you need to prioritize is your family. Honor your husband, honor your wife. There is no such thing as life balance. When you love what you are doing, sometimes you work 8 hours, sometimes more. Some seasons involve travel. Prioritize time with your spouse. Tell them you love them. Be intentional.

Schedule a date night with your spouse. Honor your children.

To let her know I was thinking about her, I sent my wife, Mari, silly text messages during a recent trip to London, England. As I traveled to Asia, I sent her videos so she could experience the trip with me. That was my way of honoring her and letting her know that I love her.

Schedule a date night with your spouse. Honor your children. We often want to tell our children what to do but that is the wrong approach. I had to do that with my son, Julian when he began making decisions for himself. When he got into high school, I wanted him to play football. He wanted to be in the band. I really did not want him to but it was not my life to live. Sometimes we want to live our lives through our children. They do not have the same personality or giftings as we do. Then we wonder why they disengage and are miserable.

I love doing our corporate training on personalities. Men and women are brought to tears when they begin to understand the four dominant personalities and they realize how every one of them communicates differently. Your personality is part of your DNA the same way I'm Hispanic or in the same way that you might have blue eyes. I often ask participants what is going through their minds to touch them so deeply. I've heard spouses say they finally understand why their partner does the things that they do. They gain new insights about their co-workers and family members. Understanding your own personality opens up a whole new understanding of the world around you.

The last thing you need to prioritize involves your business. I'm going to share with you the one factor that shifted my thinking the most. This one thing helped set Daniel Gomez apart and really grew our brand, *Sticker Shock*, to be one of the top speaking academies in the country and soon-to-be in the world. This blew up our podcast, *The Daniel Gomez Inspires Show,* and took our *Shield of Faith Business and Executive Coaching* to another level. All our book publishing services and our podcast launching services grew! Do you want to know what this "one thing is?" Prioritizing my life. Putting God first. Honoring my wife and my children. And then my business.

Write this down in your notebook:
God.
Family.
Business.

I can guarantee you that when you prioritize in the correct order, things are going to start changing for the better in your life and in your business. This is my personal key to the makings of a millionaire mind. Above all else, this is what helped me get to the next level.

You are not of the world economy. You are of God's economy.

Close your eyes. Visualize you're moving your life and business from the world's economy to God's economy. There is no lack. There is no scarcity. There are no limitations in God's economy. Envision yourself living in God's economy, an economy of abundance. Envision your revenue growing because you are putting God first. You are honoring your family and putting them second. The business is flourishing because you are prioritizing your life and you've done all these things right.

Spend the first 30 to 45 minutes with God each day, reading his word. Envision new clients onboarding. If you have a brick-and-mortar, envision more people walking through your front doors. Envision your restaurant growing. You are of God's economy. Open your eyes.

MILLIONAIRE AFFIRMATIONS

"I am of God's economy.
I declare I am putting God first in everything that I do.
God is my CEO.
I am a millionaire.
God's wealth is chasing me down.
God's blessings are chasing me down."

I will see you in the next money file.

Money File #12
MILLIONAIRES BELIEVE THEY MANIFEST THEIR OWN LIFE

Millionaires believe they manifest their own life.
Poor-minded people believe life just happens.

How many times have you heard someone say that? Life just happens and we have no say in it. I've heard countless people make that comment and fully believe it to be true. In reality, it is false. Life does not just happen. Life is what we make of it. Life is what we do with it. Life is what we create of it.

Millionaires believe they manifest their own life. Millionaires believe that they are the architect of their lives. Let's look at an architect. What does an architect do? An architect designs buildings. An architect decides what colors that building is going to be, what materials the building will be made of. An architect decides how many stories high the structure is going to be and designs the foundation to support that building. That building does not exist in and of itself. The only existence that the building has is that which the architect creates.

I want you to understand that you are the architect of your life. You are the architect that is designing your life daily.

What type of life are you creating for yourself? What are you building for yourself? What type of life are you manifesting?

 Pull out your notebook and write down the areas of your life that you are guilty of believing "life just happens."

One of the biggest lies I've heard is "Well, it was just not meant to be." No, sometimes you are just not taking action. Sometimes you are taking the wrong action or making the wrong decision. In life, the wrong actions that you take, or even the actions that you never took, are what created your life as it is today. Right now, you are living the decisions that you made 3-5 years ago. The choices that you made; you are living them right now.

You have to embody the idea that millionaires believe that they manifest their own life. You are a millionaire from this day forward. That is to be your mindset. Ask yourself "Is this choice and decision that I am making right now, at this moment, moving me closer to the life that I want, or is it moving me away?"

The decisions and choices that you make daily determine whether you go forward or backward. If you are not moving towards the life that you want, then you know you are making the wrong choice. Millionaires understand that every decision that they make is sowing a seed that will manifest in their future. You, my friend, have the makings of a millionaire mind inside of you. You have to get away from the stinking thinking that says life just happens. Because it does not.

 Get out your notebook. Write these two questions down:
• Are the choices that I am making today moving me towards my goals and the life that I want or are

these choices moving me away?

- Are the decisions that I am making today moving me towards the future that I desire or are they moving me away?

It is that simple. Sometimes we make it much more complicated because of our poor-minded financial inner economy. The process of becoming and having that millionaire-minded financial inner economy is to have the life that you dream of, the life that you deserve, a life of abundance. The limitless life.

The decisions and choices that you make daily determine whether you go forward or backward.

Close your eyes. Envision yourself making the right decisions. I want you to feel yourself making the decisions that are moving you towards a future that you desire. Do you feel yourself winning? Do you see yourself graduating from college? Do you see yourself buying that dream house because of the choices and decisions that you are making today? No longer are you going backward.

It feels amazing just to feel good about yourself and the decisions and choices that you are making. You are winning and celebrating those wins. Take a moment and enjoy this feeling. Envision the results that you wanted. Envision the life you desire, that you are building because you are the architect of your life. Doesn't it feel amazing? Feel yourself gripping the steering wheel of that new dream car you've always wanted.

Open your eyes.

MILLIONAIRE AFFIRMATIONS

"I am manifesting the life that I want.
I am creating the life that I desire.
Every decision that I make is bringing me closer and
closer to my dreams.
Every choice that I make is drawing me closer to my
desired outcome.
I am a millionaire.
I am super-rich.
I am worthy and deserving of God's best."

It's not easy, ladies and gentlemen.

I will see you in Part 3.

PART 3

BUILD YOUR MILLIONAIRE LIFE

BRICK #1:
FOCUS ON WHO YOU ARE BECOMING

Welcome to Part 3 of *The Makings of a Millionaire Mind*, Build Your Millionaire Life.

First of all, I want to congratulate you on making it to this section of the book. I want you to focus on the person that you are becoming. Becoming a millionaire is more than just the financial aspect. You are becoming a person who celebrates others. You are becoming a person who is amazing. You are becoming a person of integrity, of great character.

Having money is a great part of being a millionaire. I enjoy spending money just like the next person. I enjoy the finer things in life. But it is really the person that I have become these past five years that has brought fulfillment to my life. I enjoy being able to be a blessing to all the people around me, whether it is hiring the employees that we have, the vendors we use, or pouring into the contractors that help us to make all our clients' dreams come true. No one person can do it by themselves.

Poor-minded people think they can do it by themselves. That was Daniel Gomez. I thought that I could do it all by myself. I was leery because of the hurts that I have gone through being backstabbed and betrayed. I was talked about by people that I had poured time and money into. I have had people that I welcomed into our home turn and walk away spreading negativity about me. It hurts. I am a human just the same as you are. But the grand prize is the person that I have developed into while becoming a millionaire.

 Get out your notebook and write down the answer to these questions:
- How have you changed since you started reading this book?
- What notes have you taken that have helped you make lasting changes as a person?
- Which aspect of this book has really spoken to you?
- Which money file hit close to home for you?

The truth is, we all have a path to become the millionaire we were destined to be. We're going to all use our own unique ingredients because we are all unique in our own way. We all carry our own unique DNA and personalities. We all bring to the table our own individual culture and history. We all have the same core ingredient but each of us has our own unique toppings. Be unique to who you are on this journey to becoming the millionaire that God created you to be. Celebrate yourself. Celebrate that you have made it this far. Build your millionaire life.

 Write in your notebook:
- List five changes that you have seen in yourself since you began reading *The Makings of a Millionaire Mind*.
- What are five differences that you have noticed within yourself?
- Has anyone around you noticed something different about you?

Sometimes as we are going through a transformation, we don't see it in ourselves. Sometimes it is difficult to see the transformation from our own point of view. If you have been putting in the work, reading each section twice and taking notes, going back and studying the parts of the book that spoke to you, you are changing. Remember, you cannot rush the process. You have to trust the process of who you are becoming.

For me, I have become more loving and patient with my wife and children. I have been communicating with them on a deeper level. I am building quality relationships with my immediate family as well as with people around me that I meet at conferences or events. I am being intentional in building quality relationships with quality people in this season of my life.

Building long-lasting relationships with people who celebrate me and I, in return, celebrate them. This brings me the deepest joy right now. Take a moment and list the five changes that you have seen in yourself.

BRICK #2:
BRICK BY BRICK

The foundation has been laid. You have worked to establish the foundation. You have dealt with the shame. You have dealt with the guilt. You have grown tremendously.

I want you to notice how you have transformed and are not the same person anymore. You are happier and you are a new human being. Now that the foundation has been laid, it is time to start building your millionaire life brick by brick. As you build, keep in mind that there are going to be days when you are discouraged. There will be days that you want to give up. You will get frustrated. I know this from experience. I had days like this.

One evening I was talking to my wife, Mari, feeling very discouraged. As I was going from one level of success to another, I was growing out of my comfort zone. It felt like so much was on top of me weighing down on me at that moment. I broke down in tears and I asked her, "What is all this for? Is it really worth it?" My wife started praying for me and reassured me "Honey, it is going to be okay."

As you start to build upward, every brick is going to be different. The beautiful part is that you do not have to figure everything out. God has it already figured out. In those moments of doubt, those moments when fear wants to set in and challenges you and tells you that you can't do this, I want you to know that you can. I am reminding you that it is possible for you.

You are reading this book for a reason. You did not pick it up by chance. God already knew. He already had this book in your path. The same way he had already put it in your path is the same way that he has everything figured out for you. Pride and ego are sometimes hard to let go of. We don't realize how deep down into our soul and into our core they exist. I can tell you that I surrendered and realized that God is my source for everything. That's when the breakthroughs happened for me in becoming a millionaire.

In those moments of doubt, those moments when fear wants to set in and challenges you and tells you that you can't do this, I want you to know that you can. I am reminding you that it is possible for you.

When you are having a rough evening and you feel like you want to give up, just know that God is going to take you by the hand and walk right beside you. If you would have told me 5 years ago that DG Enterprises was going to be publishing books, launching podcasts, producing podcasts for others or that I was going to be an executive and business coach, or that we were going to be developing speakers through the *Sticker Shock Speaking Academy*, I would have thought you were crazy.

But I am doing it. I am doing it with God's help. God is there to help you, too.

As you are building upwards, I want you to see yourself as a skyscraper. See yourself as a beautiful skyscraper, lighting up the night in the city skyline. You are making a difference in your city, in your state, and around the globe because you dared to be different from the masses. You dared to stand out. You did not back down and dim your light when others shared their uninvited opinions.

Build up with confidence knowing that the dream of becoming a millionaire is possible for you. I want you to challenge all the doubts that come into your mind. The greatest salesperson in the world is doubt. You are stronger than the doubt because you are seeing the results show up in your life.

Close your eyes. Envision yourself as a beautiful skyscraper shining bright, pointing to the heavens and adding value to everyone who comes in contact with you. You are the skyscraper that pours into people financially. You are the skyscraper that is making the difference in people's lives because you have the wealth and capabilities to do so.

Your capacity has expanded to receive more so that you may do more for the world.

Doesn't it feel amazing to be a majestic skyscraper adding value to the marketplace and to the people around you?

Brick #3:
Live Generously

One of the best aspects of being a millionaire is that we are able to live generously. We are able to give and help to support the homeless, the needy, and various ministries around the world. We can help support our community right here in San Antonio, Texas. As I embark on the journey of believing that this was possible for me, God reminded me that the wealth that we are building is not just for Daniel. It is not even for my family. It is for a cause bigger than us.

Millionaires are generous. Millionaires are givers. Do you give a tithe of 10% to your church? Pouring into God's kingdom was a game-changer in building our wealth. It is a great feeling when you give with a cheerful heart. On the hard days, and everybody has hard days, I would force myself to find someone that I could pour into and bless. For some reason, we have this crazy idea that giving will cause our bank accounts to run short. I was guilty of falling into that scarcity mindset at times. As God conditions and trains, you to give hundreds, he takes it to the next level and challenges you to give thousands, and then to give ten thousand. As he was stretching my capacity to give, I was fearful that I would not have enough.

I learned that God's shovel is bigger than my shovel. As I was shoveling out the blessings, God was shoveling to fill up my bank account even more. The Book of Wisdom says, "When we sow a seed of generosity, that seed comes back 30, 60, 100-fold." Sowing the seed requires faith because many times our own intellect fails us. If God prompts your heart, know that it is the holy spirit moving on you to give. Don't be scared.

I can say with confidence that God has been faithful in our lives to honor those seeds of generosity that were sown. In 2019, while I was in prayer, God said "Daniel, you want to be a millionaire, don't you? Then why haven't you sewn a million-dollar seed?" I was caught off guard. In my mind, I had been giving faithfully with what he had given me, but I had never given a million-dollar seed.

That was a very scary moment in my life. We had never given one lump sum that large. I remember prayerfully deciding with my wife to give $1,000,000. We gave it in faith and God honored it. Once you do something like that one time, it is easier to do it again.

As you accumulate your wealth and your bank account balance grows, remember, that money is not just for you. It is for the people that the Lord is going to put in your path to bless. You are his hands and feet.

I'm going to challenge you right now to start being a generous giver before you get to the next level of success. Don't wait until your bank account says $1,000,000. Start your habit of giving right now. Develop the habit of generosity. Start practicing by eating meals at restaurants and picking up the tab. Get in the habit of surprising people by paying for their dinner. Choose a random table of people you don't even know and anonymously pay their bill. Start building millionaire habits. They are important bricks.

What if someone I give money to uses it for drugs or alcohol? I can tell you from my own experience if you do what God tells you to do, it is our responsibility to follow his lead. Whatever that person does with the gift you bless them with, they are the ones that have to answer to God. Answer the call when God tells you to give. Living generously has given me joy and brought fulfillment to my life. It is a great feeling.

When you can surprise people and give into their lives, it brings tears to your eyes.

When you can surprise people and give into their lives, it brings tears to your eyes.

I remember when my daughter was getting married. She had already moved out and was growing her little family. She was excited. A friend of mine suggested that I should pay for her wedding. I told him, "I don't think so. She has moved out already and she is doing her own thing. She has been out of the house for over 2 years. She's good." Coming back from Houston that evening, I was thinking about the words that my friend had spoken to me. As I went about my week, those words stayed on my mind. "Maybe I should pay for the wedding."

Later in the week, I walked into my wife's office and asked her "What do you think about us paying for our daughter's wedding?" Mari started crying. She answered, "Daniel, I have been waiting for you to say this!" We both got excited and decided to FaceTime our daughter right then and there. She was driving so we asked her to pull over to the side of the road for a moment.

She got very concerned asking us what was wrong. I'll never forget her reaction when I had told her that we would be paying for her wedding. She began crying. It brought healing to her soul. She could not believe it. That was one of the most joyful moments of my life.

Years ago, the old Daniel was not very nice at times when it came to making decisions about the money. We don't realize sometimes how much pain we cause to our spouses and children. God used that decision to pay for her wedding, to bring healing to her. I can tell you that since then, our relationship has blossomed like a beautiful rose. She reaches out to me, and we communicate in ways we have never communicated. We have a true father-daughter relationship filled with love.

As you are accumulating your wealth, know that God is entrusting you with a responsibility to let it flow through you and not to hoard it.

Ladies and gentlemen, that is the power of generosity. As you are accumulating your wealth, know that God is entrusting you with a responsibility to let it flow through you and not to hoard it. Of course, you can keep a portion for yourself, but it is to be the hands and feet of God.

BRICK #4:
ATTITUDE OF GRATITUDE

As the wins start to appear in our lives and we begin to stack them, it can be easy to become ungrateful. When we become ungrateful, it can be easy to start taking people for granted.

I remember the day that my wife called me, and I could barely understand what she was saying. She was crying hysterically. I was trying to console her and calm her down so I could understand her. The only words that I could make out between the sobs were "breast cancer."

In one moment, my entire life changed. For the first time in a very long time, I did not have an answer. I had held some very prestigious titles and been quite successful in the automotive industry. Our house was paid off and we had a nice little nest egg in the bank. But I realized at that moment that I had been taking my wife for granted without even seeing it. My titles, my prominence, my bank account nor my success were going to be able to help my wife survive the biggest fight of her life. I remember telling her to go home and we would figure it out together.

The truth is, I had no idea what to do. I remember going down the highway towards home and noticing that the check engine light was on. I remember God saying to my heart "Son, the check engine light in your life has been on for a long time. You just failed to acknowledge it."

As I drove into our neighborhood, I saw my wife's car in the driveway. I did not know what words to say when I walked through the door. I just remember embracing her as we stood crying together, releasing those emotions of fear, worry, and doubt. I remember telling my wife that while I did not know what to do, God did.

That is where my life changed.

Cancer has a way of quickly humbling a person.

I called on the faith that I once had back in my younger days. I was scared. What was I going to tell my teenage son? I know what it is like not to have a mother. My mom died when I was 10 years old. It sucks. I remember crying out for God to help us and heal my wife.

And he did!

It was the longest journey of our lives together. Eight major surgeries. A double mastectomy. It was a hard road to recovery for my wife. I can tell you the lessons that I learned as a man, as a husband, and as a father were priceless. I became very aware of how ungrateful I had become in my life.

I was so selfish and focused on Daniel Gomez that I failed to realize how blessed I was for many years. God had given us good health, a beautiful family, and success in our careers. Those lessons that I learned on my wife's journey to recovery from breast cancer were invaluable. I have used many of those lessons in business and I still use them today. Those lessons helped to make me the man, the husband, and the father that I am today.

Cancer has a way of quickly humbling a person. Nothing brings down a person faster than pride. I learned that when I humbled myself, I was more receptive to what life was trying to teach me. You may be reading this right now and not be aware that you might be like the old Daniel Gomez; prideful, arrogant, selfish know-it-all, thinking that you have it all figured out.

I am here to tell you out of love, get over yourself. Don't be Daniel Gomez. Don't be so stubborn that it takes a crisis to open your eyes and heart to realize how ungrateful you have become over the years.

I quickly learned not to take my wife or children for granted.

 Grab your notebook and think about some things you may be taking for granted. Be honest with yourself. Who or what have you not been grateful for?

Gratitude is the key to more. Gratitude is the key to promotion. If you cannot be grateful for the level of success that you are experiencing right now, and if you cannot be grateful for the blessings that have been bestowed on you, how do you expect to be grateful for more?

This is one of the huge blocks that I see when coaching my clients. It is a core problem. Many times, we focus on the symptom when we need to go to the source of the issue. We focus on the fruit when we need to focus on the root. The root of our problem is often ingratitude.

Take a moment and write down what you need to be more grateful for in your life. Tomorrow is never promised. In order to be trusted with more, you have to appreciate what you have been given. Many people do not reach millionaire status because of their lack of gratitude.

Don't let this be you. I tell you this from the road I traveled myself these past five years. There is more out there for you but you have to appreciate what you have right now, at this moment. There really is an abundance waiting for you. The millionaire life is out there for you to live. There is nothing wrong with being wealthy or having success in your life.

One of the key factors in reaching this level of success is being grateful and having a joyful heart for what you currently have.

One of the key factors in reaching this level of success is being grateful and having a joyful heart for what you currently have. Take care of the little and I promise you it will multiply and grow.

Close your eyes. Envision yourself being more grateful for what you have. Feel the gratitude coursing through your veins as you picture the important things in your life. Be grateful for the vehicle that you have. It may not be a Lamborghini or Porsche, but you do not have to ride a bus to work, do you? Feel that gratitude.

Envision yourself being filled with joy and gratitude for the house that you live in. You did not have to spend last night sleeping on the street. Feel the love for those around you and be grateful that you have friends and family that you care about and who care about you.

Feel the Holy Spirit filling you up with joy. Gratitude is just pouring out of you.

Whisper "Thank you, thank you, thank you." Doesn't it feel amazing to appreciate what you have? Gratitude is one of the

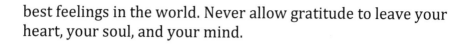
best feelings in the world. Never allow gratitude to leave your heart, your soul, and your mind.

BRICK #5:
PROTECT YOUR HEART

If we have an attitude of gratitude and a joyful heart as all of this success and wealth comes your way and as you transition from a poor-minded financial inner economy to a millionaire-minded financial inner economy, you do not want to implode. So many millionaires self-destruct when they hit millionaire status. This is the exact reason why so many do not move on to the multi-millionaire level.

On this journey, you need to protect your heart. Once you begin gaining more prominence and significance, you need to protect your heart. It is written "The issues of life flow from our heart." But what does that mean?

I am speaking from experience. As the wealth grows, as the bank account grows, there is a temptation to hoard money. You are tempted to stop doing the things which got you to this level of success. I'm being completely transparent with you when I tell you that greed wants to sneak in. There is an old saying in the Book of Wisdom "It is the little foxes that destroy the vineyard."

Those little foxes sometimes show up in the form of greed. I think one of the lies that we have been told is that "money magnifies who you are." I used to believe this statement to the core. As I started elevating and accumulating wealth, I realized over 90% of people live in lack and scarcity. They have never had a million dollars. They have never had this level of wealth and money so how do they know how to respond to it? I think it is an unfair statement.

It takes intentionality to protect your heart and to keep doing the daily activities which elevated you to this level of wealth and success. Keep being generous. Keep reading and practicing the money files. Keep applying all the wisdom you have learned earlier in this book. It is a never-ending process. There are always new heights to achieve and new levels to reach. Protect your heart at all times. It will benefit you greatly in all areas of your life.

> *It is a never-ending process. There are always new heights to achieve and new levels to reach.*

Money is meant to move. When I lead corporate trainings, I used the word currency instead of money. I explain that when you see money just as money, it is equal to a stagnant pond. What do you think of when you think of a stagnant pond? A smelly, stinky collection of water that does not move and has no life in it. It looks dirty and you cannot see through it. I know I wouldn't dare swim in it! Would you?

When you look at the word "currency" - the Latin root of the word is the same root word for current. Imagine the currents of the Colorado River. It is moving, powerful, fresh, and invigorating. This is what money is supposed to be. It is supposed to be moving. Start referring to money as currency, and envision it moving and blessing those who need it. Now this is the type of water I would definitely swim in.

Wealth was created to help people. Wealth was created to make a difference in people's lives. It was never created for us to be greedy and hoard. It was created to be distributed and help set people free around the world. Wealth can do so much good for our communities.

If you feel like the money is controlling you and becoming your master, I encourage you to bless somebody and give it away. Do you remember earlier in the book when I challenged you to carry five $100 bills? Bless somebody with that money. Don't let greed become part of who you are. Protect your heart at all times. At all costs.

See yourself as the loving, generous millionaire. The whole reason I wrote this book was to help people develop the right attitude and the right approach to becoming a millionaire God's way. I want you to succeed in your relationships and in your life as you are making a difference in the lives of those around you. I want to guide you towards being the caring and loving human being you were created to be and impact the world.

Close your eyes. Envision money as currency. Whenever you see a picture of a river, remind yourself this is what money is supposed to be like. It is currency, always moving, flowing to you and through you to bless others.

BRICK #6:
KEEP BUILDING

I want to encourage you to keep building a life of abundance and wealth. *The Makings of a Millionaire Mind* has given you all the ingredients needed to live a life of happiness, joy, abundance, wealth, and increase. All that you need is within you now.

You have put in the work. You have invested the time. You have conquered the mountain. Stand tall, raise your arms and do your victory dance. Celebrate yourself. Soak in the win, soak in the victory. Be grateful for all of your accomplishments. Gratitude is key.

A quick word of warning: I do not want you to get comfortable. That was a mistake that I made. I got comfortable for a season. I started to plateau, and God began to send me to higher levels. Once you hit a threshold and have a certain amount of money in your bank account, you might be tempted to slack off a bit. I want to encourage you to keep pushing and keep going. Keep building your millionaire life.

I have learned that if we are not progressing, we are regressing. If we are not growing, we are dying. Stay creative because when you are not creating, you are disintegrating.

You do not want to plateau or start going backward in life. It can easily happen if you are not intentional. I have seen many people who have reached the millionaire status waste all the work and effort that they put into reaching that level of success and prominence. They stopped doing the work. They accumulated wealth, success, and riches like they never had before, and they went into horde mode. They forget to be givers. They begin to cling to everything they have. That is the worst decision you can make.

Write this down in your journal right now. Don't stop doing what got you here. Keep investing in yourself and keep growing. "When you are green, you grow. When you are ripe, you rot." I heard that years ago when I was very young and entering the automotive industry. I do not want you to rot. I want you to keep growing and making a difference in the world.

Never stop learning. Keep taking in new information. Take action and be bold every day. Be decisive.

Share this book with everyone around you. Not only is it going to help them with their finances, but it will also help heal pains and issues that they have carried for years. This book will be a blessing to them.

I want you to visit our website: www.TheMakingsofaMillionaireMind.com to accelerate your results even more. Invest in our online program that consists of 27 powerful modules with 22 money files. There are 10 additional money files that are not in this book. They will make a difference in how fast you accelerate towards the makings of your millionaire mind.

The feedback has been amazing. We have helped hundreds of people so far. I want you to be one of them. Make this investment in yourself and get our online course, *The Makings of a Millionaire Mind.*

I would love to see you at one of our live *The Makings of a Millionaire Mind* workshops where we do live, in-person exercises together. God shows up in these events and brings miraculous healing and deliverance from depression, addiction, anxiety, and fear. We have seen major breakthroughs at our events. People open up and allow themselves to be restored.

I am honored that you have joined me on this journey and that you have allowed me to help you in the makings of your millionaire mind. I look forward to seeing you in our course and I look forward to seeing you at one of our live workshops.

Make a small investment in yourself and it will pay back huge dividends.

Thank you once again for doing the work in yourself.

This is Daniel Gomez Inspires saying "if nobody has ever told you that they believe in you, I'm telling you right now 'I believe in you.' Your best is yet to come."

Daniel would be honored to speak at your event.
He's also available to train and coach your organization.

Visit us at www.DanielGomezSpeaker.com
Email us at Daniel@DanielGomezSpeaker.com

Call us at (210) 663-5954 to book Daniel today!

Made in the USA
Columbia, SC
03 October 2024